Praise for *Faith*

"*The Year of Faith . . . the New E__ ___ ___...... are just slogans if we do not first appreciate the truth, beauty, and wisdom of what we believe. How to do that? Start with this crisp yet compelling book by Cardinal Wuerl on the Creed!"
—**Cardinal Timothy M. Dolan**, Archbishop of New York.

"Clear, concise, confident, and a certain sign that the renewal of catechesis is truly underway, Cardinal Wuerl's *Faith That Transforms Us* is a must-use resource for preaching and teaching the faith and an essential tool for the New Evangelization."
—**Very Rev. Robert Barron**, creator of the Catholicism series, founder of Word on Fire Catholic Ministries, and Rector/President of Mundelein Seminary/University of St. Mary of the Lake, Illinois

"Every Catholic will benefit from Cardinal Wuerl's insightful and practical reflections on the articles of the Creed. Not only will we understand more clearly what we believe, but we will know how to apply our beliefs to how we live our lives. This book makes a significant contribution to restoring clarity and confidence to Catholics regarding both the truthfulness and relevance of our foundational beliefs."
—**Ralph Martin**, President, Renewal Ministries, and author of *Will Many Be Saved? What Vatican II Actually Teaches and Its Implications for the New Evangelization*

"For any Catholic who has ever felt that they were just going through the motions at Mass, or for any Catholic desiring a deeper appreciation of our core beliefs, this book is for you. Cardinal Wuerl, as a teacher and shepherd, knows some of the struggles Christians face in today's frenetic and noisy world. *Faith That Transforms Us*, with

its practical and very readable format and helpful discussion questions, will do just that. Through a better understanding of the Creed, this book will transform your Mass experience and bring you closer to Christ and his Church."
—**Teresa Tomeo,** Catholic author and syndicated talk show host

"Every Sunday we publicly profess the Creed. Cardinal Wuerl offers a powerful reminder that our faith, while very personal, must never remain private. We must believe what we profess, we must understand what we believe, and we must act upon what we understand. Our belief in Jesus Christ is a *Faith That Transforms Us.*
—**Curtis Martin,** President and founder, FOCUS—The Fellowship of Catholic University Students

"With the aid of *Faith That Transforms Us* by Cardinal Donald Wuerl, believers have the potential to move beyond rote recitation of the simple words we speak in the Creed to embracing in our hearts the truths that lie at the core of our faith. A perfect resource for life-long Catholics who long for a deeper connection to Christ and his Church or for those who seek to know more about the beliefs we profess, Cardinal Wuerl's book belongs in every home and parish."
—**Lisa M. Hendey,** founder of CatholicMom.com and author of *A Book of Saints for Catholic Moms*

"Cardinal Wuerl offers Catholics a powerfully simple reflection on a few words—but not just any words. These are words that open hearts and minds to the immense depths of our faith: the Nicene Creed. Through this deep and profound yet clear and straightforward reflection, we can find life, and find it more abundantly."
—**Helen Osman,** Secretary of Communications, United States Conference of Catholic Bishops

FAITH THAT TRANSFORMS US

Reflections on the Creed

Cardinal Donald Wuerl
Archbishop of Washington

Published by The Word Among Us Press
7115 Guilford Drive
Frederick, Maryland 21704

17 14 15 14 13   1 2 3 4 5
ISBN: 978-1-59325-244-1
eISBN: 978-1-59325-449-0

Library of Congress Control Number: 2012954746

CONTENTS

The Nicene Creed

I believe in one God,
the Father almighty,
maker of heaven and earth,
of all things visible and invisible.

I believe in one Lord Jesus Christ,
the Only Begotten Son of God,
born of the Father before all ages.
God from God, Light from Light,
true God from true God,
begotten, not made, consubstantial with the Father;
through him all things were made.
For us men and for our salvation
he came down from heaven,
and by the Holy Spirit was incarnate of the Virgin Mary,
and became man.
For our sake he was crucified under Pontius Pilate,
he suffered death and was buried,
and rose again on the third day
in accordance with the Scriptures.
He ascended into heaven
and is seated at the right hand of the Father.
He will come again in glory
to judge the living and the dead
and his kingdom will have no end.

I believe in the Holy Spirit, the Lord, the giver of life,
who proceeds from the Father and the Son,
who with the Father and the Son is adored and glorified,
who has spoken through the prophets.

I believe in one, holy, catholic and apostolic Church.
I confess one Baptism for the forgiveness of sins
and I look forward to the resurrection of the dead
and the life of the world to come. Amen.

Divine Revelation

Every Sunday at Mass, we recite the words of the Nicene Creed. Each of us makes a personal and public commitment of faith, in the presence of our neighbors. We say, "I believe" to a rather long list of demanding propositions. "I believe . . . "

- in one God who is three divine persons;

- in a fatherly God who relates to me as his child;

- in a God who became man;

- in a God who continues to act through the Church;

- in a God who will raise me, body and soul, from the dead.

When we stop to think about any one of these propositions, we can identify with the man in the Gospel who "cried out" to Jesus, "I do believe, help my unbelief!" (Mark 9:24). For we know, as that man knew, that we all need help. The truths of our faith are demanding. They are more than words, more than boxes we must check so that we can call ourselves Catholic. They are living truths that are meant to make a difference in our lives.

We refer to the truths of faith as *divine revelation*. God has *revealed* them to us, because we could never arrive at them without divine help. We could devote ourselves to study over several lifetimes and never, for example, come to the conclusion that God is one and yet three: Father, Son, and Holy Spirit. By reason alone we might conclude, after much consideration, that God exists, but even then it would require time and effort, meditation and research; and our conclusions, in the end, would be tentative and prone to error. By nature we gather knowledge through our bodily senses—sight, hearing, touch, taste, and smell—but these faculties are limited to the material world and cannot perceive the spiritual.

God reveals divine mysteries to accommodate our human weakness. When we look to Jesus Christ, we look to God's perfect self-revelation. Everything we need to know for our salvation, everything we desire to know for our comfort and consolation, everything we hope for our supernatural fulfillment—it all has been revealed in Jesus Christ.

Again, it is not primarily about words. It is not just about propositions. Jesus came to earth not simply to publish information. In fact, as far as we know, he never wrote anything except something undecipherable on the ground (John 8:6, 8).

What he did come to do was to offer us a share in his divine life (2 Peter 1:4). The *Catechism of the Catholic Church* makes an important distinction between, on the one hand, the words we profess when we say, "I believe," and, on the other hand, the mysteries represented by those words.

We do not believe in formulas, but in those realities they express, which faith allows us to touch. "The believer's act [of faith] does not terminate in the propositions, but in the realities [which they express]" (St. Thomas Aquinas, *Summa Theologiae* II-II, 1, 2, *ad* 2). All the same, we do approach these realities with the help of formulations of the faith which permit us to express the faith and to hand it on, to celebrate it in community, to assimilate and live on it more and more. (CCC 170)

Every single revelation of God can be life changing and transforming when we understand it, live it out, and share it with others. Like God, we are not merely communicating information. We are sharing life.

Nevertheless, words are very important to life. God made us to communicate with words; and from divine revelation, we know that God has existed from all eternity as "the Word." So John's Gospel begins: "In the beginning was the Word, / and the Word was with God, / and the Word was God" (1:1). We are verbal because we are people mysteriously made in God's image. If words were not important to faith, you would not have read this far in this book, and I would not have written it.

In this book we use words to examine words—the articles of the Church's creed. By means of these words, we, like our ancestors in the Christian faith, draw closer to the divine Word, to Jesus Christ. We draw closer to heaven because in Christ, heaven has come to earth.

That is the faith that Christians have proclaimed since Jesus ascended to heaven. We call it the gospel, which means "good news." The mysteries of our faith are indeed mysterious, but they are a positive, uplifting, and joyful message. In the chapters that follow, we will explore the basic truths of the Catholic faith, as expressed in the Nicene Creed, to discover the abundant life they represent.

· · · · · · ·

For Christians, a creed is a summary of who Jesus is and what he does. It is a compact statement of belief. It comes from the Latin word *credo*, which means "I believe."

Christians have always used such formulas to express their faith. We find them even in the New Testament in compact phrases such as "Jesus is Lord" (Romans 10:9; 1 Corinthians 12:3). With a minimal number of words, creeds convey deep theological truths; in the case of "Jesus is Lord," it is the mystery of Jesus' divinity. St. Paul taught that such public statements are an important part of our life and our salvation.

> "The word is near you, / in your mouth and in your heart" (that is, the word of faith that we preach), for, if you confess with your mouth that Jesus is Lord and believe in your heart that God raised him from the dead, you will be saved. For one believes with the heart and so is justified, and one confesses with the mouth and so is saved. For the scripture says, "No one who believes in him will be put to shame." (Romans 10:8-11)

We want the words of the public statements we call creeds to be in our hearts as well as on our lips. Only then can we be truly transformed. We want to study the propositions so that we may embrace the mysteries. This book is designed as a guide for that process of discovery.

Each chapter focuses on a section of the Nicene Creed and approaches it through a series of questions:

1. What is the revelation? (Here I'll provide a representative passage from Scripture.)

2. What does it mean?

3. How can this truth transform me?

4. How do I live it?

5. How do I share it with others?

Each chapter will end with discussion questions as well as references for further study, a "Looking for more?" section that points to relevant passages in Scripture, the Church's catechisms, and other Church documents.

• • • • • • •

"And the apostles said to the Lord, 'Increase our faith'" (Luke 17:5). It is an echo of the cry we heard earlier. Only then, it came from a man in dire need. Now it comes from Jesus' inner circle. Even they feel the need for greater faith. Even they sense that they're probably not up to the task of responding in faith as they must. So they make the request: "Lord, increase our faith."

This book is all about increasing our faith. So we should begin by making the apostles' prayer our own.

For faith itself—and any increase of faith—can only come to us as a grace from God. The ability to accept Jesus' lordship is a gift, and we should be thankful for it. Nevertheless, God respects our spiritual freedom. We are free to accept the gift or reject it, to cultivate it or neglect it. Only free creatures can love. Animals cannot, and neither can machines. God made us free so that we could respond in love to his gift of faith.

When we speak of *faith*, we use the word in two ways, really. We use it to speak of the act by which we place our trust in God. We accept God's word; we accept Jesus. We "have faith." Some people call this trust a "leap" of faith, because there is no way to prove that it is actually God who is speaking to us. We can cite evidence and point to the authority of reputable people—saints and scholars—but we're never going to be able to demonstrate with mathematical precision that the Almighty has spoken to us in revelation. We choose to trust God's ways of communicating.

But *faith* has another sense. We use the term to mean, not only the *act* of believing, but also the *facts* we believe in. Thus, we speak of "the Catholic faith," or simply "the faith."

It is one thing to say, "I place my faith in Jesus. I believe him." But faith requires more. Faith requires us to ask the follow-up question: *Well, what did Jesus say? What is the content of the faith that he revealed and taught?* And that brings us back to the Creed.

• • • • • • •

The Church has many creeds. They are concise summaries of the revealed doctrines that are most central to Christianity.

Though they all summarize the same faith, they were composed for different purposes. The Apostles' Creed is very ancient and served for the baptismal instruction of converts in the early church of Rome. It is very brief. Today it is used most often in Masses for children. The Athanasian Creed was coined in the fourth or fifth century as an antidote to the heresies of that time. It is a rather detailed profession of the Church's faith in the Blessed Trinity and the Incarnation of the Word in Jesus Christ.

Intermediate between those two creeds—both in history and in level of detail—stands the Nicene Creed. It draws its name from the Church's first ecumenical council, the Council of Nicaea in A.D. 325. Indeed, most of its articles were drawn up by the bishops who attended that council. Additional lines were added at the First Council of Constantinople later in the same century, in 381. So its full name is sometimes rendered as the *Niceno-Constantinopolitan Creed*. But to most of us, most of the time, it is simply "the Creed," because it is the one most commonly recited at Mass on Sundays and holy days.

The Creed is our framework for passing on the story of our salvation. It is a distillation of the Bible and the apostolic tradition—but it is not the whole story. As St. John said at the end of his Gospel: "There are also many other things that Jesus did, but if these were to be described individually, I do not think the whole world would contain the books that would be written" (John 21:25).

The Creed, however, stands for the whole of the faith. When we recite it publicly in church, we are making a commitment. We are doing essentially what new Catholics do on the day they enter into full communion with the Church. They say, "I believe and profess all that the holy Catholic Church believes, teaches, and proclaims to be revealed by God." That is the meaning of our recitation of the Creed every Sunday.

Authentic Catholic faith is never partial or selective; it is always universal. We say yes to the whole mystery of faith and to each of its elements. We do this because of our personal faith in God. We believe the truth that God reveals because we believe God, and we believe that God is still teaching in and through the Church. When Peter came to recognize that Jesus was the Christ, the Son of the living God, he was prepared to believe any word of Jesus, for it was clear to him that God is always to be believed: "Master, to whom shall we go? You have the words of eternal life. We have come to believe and are convinced that you are the Holy One of God" (John 6:68-69).

"Words of eternal life" can come only from "the Holy One of God"—the God who made us and who has the power to change us in ways that fulfill us, complete us, and make us truly happy. "All of us, gazing with unveiled face on the glory of the Lord, are being transformed into the same image from glory to glory" (2 Corinthians 3:18). God wants to transform us into the image of Christ, and he wants to transform our world into the image of his kingdom.

We all want to be transformed, and it is our faith that makes such transformation possible. We make our act of faith with the words "I believe . . ."

Chapter 1

God Our Father and His Creation

I believe in one God,
the Father almighty,
maker of heaven and earth,
of all things visible and invisible.

What is the revelation?

Jesus answered and said to them, "Amen, amen, I say to you, a son cannot do anything on his own, but only what he sees his father doing; for what he does, his son will do also. For the Father loves his Son and shows him everything that he himself does, and he will show him greater works than these, so that you may be amazed. For just as the Father raises the dead and gives life, so also does the Son give life to whomever he wishes. Nor does the Father judge anyone, but he has given all judgment to his Son, so that all may honor the Son just as they honor the Father. Whoever does not honor the Son does not honor the Father who sent him. Amen, amen, I say to you, whoever hears my word and believes in the one who sent me has eternal life and will not come to condemnation, but has passed from death to life. Amen, amen, I say to you, the hour is coming and is now here when the dead will hear the voice of the Son of God, and those who hear will live. For just as the Father has life in himself, so also he gave to his Son the possession of life in himself. And he gave him power to exercise judgment, because he is the Son of Man. Do not be amazed at this, because the hour is coming in which all who are in the tombs will hear his voice and will come out, those who have done good deeds to the resurrection of life, but those who have done wicked deeds to the resurrection of condemnation.

"I cannot do anything on my own; I judge as I hear, and my judgment is just, because I do not seek my own will but the will of the one who sent me."

—The Gospel According to St. John 5:19-30

What does it mean?

The heart of the gospel is Jesus' revelation of God's fatherhood. Repeatedly, he speaks of God as Father and addresses him as "Father"—even using the intimate form of "Abba" (Mark 14:36), which is the Hebrew equivalent of "Daddy." We hardly notice such language today, especially if we live in traditionally Christian cultures. It has become like white noise. But in Jesus' day, it sounded like the opening shots of a revolution. If we read the verses that appear immediately before the discourse above, we learn that it was "for this reason"—*because* he "called God his own father"—that Jesus' adversaries "tried all the more to kill him" (John 5:18). They saw what was implicit in Jesus' words and would one day become explicit in the Creed: in calling God "Father," Jesus was claiming equality with God.

Pope Benedict XVI spoke of "two dimensions" of God's fatherhood.[1] First of all, God is Father because he is the origin of everything—"maker of all things visible and invisible." God created everything out of nothing. This is a distinctively biblical idea. When Moses encountered God in the burning bush, he asked his name. God responded, "I am who I am" (Exodus 3:14). Only God could make such a statement, because only God simply *is*. Everything else in the cosmos, everything in heaven and on earth, has been created by God and is dependent on God for its very existence. "All things came to be through him, / and without him nothing came to be" (John 1:3).

Some centuries before Christ, Greek philosophers proposed that the "stuff" of the material world was eternal. It had always been there, but one day a god took the trouble to mold that primeval matter into the universe as we know it. That account begs the question of where the primeval matter came from, and several other important questions as well.

Only the tradition of Israel proposed a true creation: something from nothing.

Because God made the world and everything in it, he could be compared to an earthly father, who certainly plays an originating role in the conception of a child. Indeed, that comparison appears several times in the Old Testament. In chapter 32 of the Book of Deuteronomy, Moses compares God to many creatures that would be familiar to his hearers. God is like a rock (verse 4), and like an eagle (verse 11), and also like a father (verse 6). Similarly, the prophet Malachi asks, "Have we not all one father? / Has not one God created us?" (2:10). God also appears as father-like in his protection of Israel (Exodus 4:22) and its king (Psalm 2:6-7). He is father to the chosen people because he has called them into being.

That is the first dimension of divine fatherhood. As creator, God is *like* a father. But Jesus' adversaries knew that he was claiming something far beyond what could be found in the words of Moses or Malachi. And that brings us to the second and more important dimension of God's fatherhood: only God is *eternally Father*. He is not simply father-like in relation to creation; he is truly *the Father* in relation to his only Son, his *eternal* Son, who is the Word made flesh, Jesus Christ. Even before creation, God was always Father because the divine Word was always his Son.

Jesus claimed an unprecedented communion with the Father. He said that, as the Son, he could claim divine prerogatives such as "judgment" (John 5:22) and the giving of life (5:21). He taught that all should "honor the Son just as they honor the Father" (5:23). St. John's Gospel opens with the stark claim that Jesus was "in the beginning with God" (1:2) and was actively involved in the world's creation (1:3). John saw Jesus' "glory as of the Father's only Son" (1:14). St. John's Gospel clearly presents Jesus as coequal and coeternal with God the Father. With such assertions, the Evangelist stepped far beyond metaphor. Divinely inspired, he set down facts that we could never have known about God's inner life: his eternal fatherhood and sonship in the unity of the Holy Spirit.

The Church would come to speak of this mystery using the term *Trinity*. It is the central mystery of the Christian faith. Father, Son, and Holy Spirit are all equal in power, all coeternal, and all divine. They differ only in that the Father is not the Son;

the Son is not the Father; the Spirit is not the Son; the Spirit is not the Father. Yet all are God; all are equal; all are coeternal; and all three are *one* in an eternal communion.

Jesus blesses his disciples with a Trinitarian formula: "in the name of the Father, and of the Son, and of the holy Spirit" (Matthew 28:19). So does St. Paul (2 Corinthians 13:13). And there are other signs of the Trinity in Scripture. When Jesus descends into the water at his baptism, for example, the bystanders hear the Father's voice and see the Holy Spirit descend as a dove (Matthew 3:16-17).

Since the earliest days, the Church's faith has been Trinitarian, and its blessings and prayers reflect this faith. We worship one God in three divine Persons. We worship three Persons in one God.

The doctrine of the Trinity is compressed into Scripture's most compact definition of God: "God is love" (1 John 4:8, 16). The Catholic author G. K. Chesterton observed that the Trinity is "simply the logical side of love." Within God himself is Someone who loves and Someone who is loved, and there is love. There is the Father and the Son, and the love they share is so profound that their love, too, is a Person: the Holy Spirit.

How can this truth transform me?

We tend to think of God in transcendent terms, as a reality far beyond us—all-powerful, all-knowing. We think of all the ways in which God is different from us. We are finite; God is infinite. We are very imperfect; God is perfect.

When Jesus came to reveal God to us, he acknowledged all those characteristics. But he told us something more. He told us that God is a father—in fact, that God can be "Our Father" (Matthew 6:9).When God became man, he chose to share our life, and he empowered us to share his life. When he taught us to pray, Jesus showed us how to take part in his own eternal conversation with the Father. As Pope Benedict put it, "Jesus thereby involves us in his own prayer; he leads us into the interior dialogue of triune love."[2] Jesus does not simply disclose information—he shares life. He brings us into communion with the Father.

Though we are imperfect and finite, we dare to call God "Our Father." We dare because Jesus told us we could, and because we are baptized into Jesus' life and so have become God's adopted children. "See what love the Father has bestowed on us that we may be called the children of God. Yet so we are" (1 John 3:1). We are children of God. This is not a metaphor or a poetic figure of speech. We really are, through the grace of the Holy Spirit, adopted children of God. We gain as a gift what only Christ has by nature. Jesus alone is the eternal Word, the eternal Son of God, and yet he has shared eternal life with us.

Nothing could be more transformative than this "divinization" of a human life. The words of the Lord's Prayer, the Holy Father explained, "aim to configure us to the image of the Son. The meaning of the Our Father goes much further than the mere provision of a prayer text. It aims to form our being, to train us in the inner attitude of Jesus (cf. Philippians 2:5)."[3]

That is what God wants for you and me. That is the meaning of our salvation. It is the most basic fact of Christian life. Pope Benedict made this point emphatically in an address to recently appointed bishops: "The fundamental gift you are called to cherish in the faithful entrusted to your pastoral care is *divine filiation*; in other words, the fact that everyone participates in Trinitarian communion. Baptism, which makes men and women 'children in the Son' and members of the church, is the root and source of all other charismatic gifts."[4]

How do I live it?

Jesus taught us to call on God as children call upon their father. He modeled such prayer for us when he called out, "Abba, Father" (Mark 14:36), using terms of endearing tenderness. He also showed us many ways to cultivate a relationship with our Father in heaven. Jesus made time to pray alone in quiet. He prayed with others and took part in ritual worship among God's people. He fasted. He did all these things, not because he needed to, but because he wanted to show us how to live on earth as children of our heavenly Father. When we live a habitual disciplined life of prayer, we are living as Jesus did, living as children of God.

We should also pray using the prayer Jesus taught us, the Lord's Prayer, the "Our Father." The early Christians used to pray it at least three times each day.

Not everyone, of course, has had a positive experience of fatherhood, and the *Catechism of the Catholic Church* and the popes have acknowledged that this can make prayer difficult. "The father's absence, the problem of a father who is not present in a child's life," said Pope Benedict, "is a serious problem of our time."[5] Yet we overcome such obstacles by drawing nearer to the perfect Father, who is in heaven. God will more than make up for the shortcomings we experience in others. We can even come to know such earthly disappointments and difficulties as occasions of greater grace, as we learn to seek in God what is lacking on earth.

How do I share it with others?

By our life and our words, we can show people that salvation is much richer than they might think. It is not just living for "the pie in the sky when you die." It is an abiding sense of confidence and well-being. Even now, even here on earth, we know "the glorious freedom of the children of God" (Romans 8:21), and Christians know this freedom even if they are imprisoned, unemployed, facing bankruptcy, or suffering rejection. It makes a powerful impression. Nothing evangelizes so effectively as an encounter with a child of God.

When we meet people who are hurting or lonely, we can do as Jesus did and model a way for them to experience God's fatherhood. Jesus also gave people words to pray so that they could get to know God as Father. We, too, can do that, handing on the very same words that Jesus gave us. Our Lord "let others in" on the loving conversation he has eternally with the Father. When we do the same, when we let others in on our conversation with God, we are living like Jesus—we are living like true children of God.

$Questions$ for reflection and discussion

1. How do you relate to God the Father? Do you see yourself as his creation? As his child? Do you see him as *your* Father?

2. What are some episodes in Jesus' life that show you how to relate to God as Father? How can you apply these in concrete ways in your own life?

3. "Within God himself is Someone who loves and Someone who is loved, and there is love." How does this description of the Trinity deepen your understanding of this mystery? How does it make you feel to know that, through Jesus, you participate in this communion of love?

4. When you think about salvation, do you usually think of it in terms of "getting into heaven"? Why is salvation much richer than that? What difference is God making in your life right now?

5. How can we "let others in" on the loving conversations we have with God? How might we, in a practical way, share what God has been doing in our lives with others?

Looking for more?

▶ In the Bible, see 1 Corinthians 8:6; Ephesians 4:4-6; Galatians 4:4-7.

▶ See the *Catechism of the Catholic Church*, 232–256 (on God's fatherhood and the Trinity), and 2777–2802 on prayer to "Our Father."

▶ See the *United States Catholic Catechism for Adults*, chapter 5, "I Believe in God."[6]

▶ See the chapter on "The Lord's Prayer" in the first volume of Pope Benedict's *Jesus of Nazareth*.[7]

▶ See Pope Benedict's discussion of "divine filiation" in his General Audience of May 23, 2012.[8]

Chapter 2

Jesus Christ, Second Person of the Trinity

> *I believe in one Lord Jesus Christ,*
> *the Only Begotten Son of God,*
> *born of the Father before all ages.*

What is the revelation?

He is the image of the invisible God,
the firstborn of all creation.
For in him were created all things in heaven and on earth,
the visible and the invisible,
whether thrones or dominions or principalities or powers;
all things were created through him and for him.
He is before all things,
and in him all things hold together.
He is the head of the body, the church.
He is the beginning, the firstborn from the dead,
that in all things he himself might be preeminent.
For in him all the fullness was pleased to dwell,
and through him to reconcile all things for him,

making peace by the blood of his cross
[through him], whether those on earth or those in heaven.

— St. Paul, Letter to the Colossians 1:15-20

And the Word became flesh
and made his dwelling among us,
and we saw his glory,
the glory as of the Father's only Son,
full of grace and truth.

— The Gospel According to St. John 1:14

What does it mean?

God strains language to the breaking point. The finite cannot contain the infinite. Human beings have coined words to describe the things they perceive with bodily senses, and the bodily senses are useless for the perception of heavenly things. "No one has ever seen God," St. John tells us at the beginning of his Gospel. No one can perceive anything spiritual with the eyes of the flesh. Yet God has made a way of approach, as John goes on to explain: "The only Son, God, who is at the Father's side, has *revealed* him" (1:18, emphasis added).

God the eternal Word makes himself approachable and accessible in human flesh and even in human words. The revelation is our meeting place. It is "the only Son"—"the Only Begotten," to use the phrase we find in the Creed—who makes this possible. God the Son has the authority and the power to do so because of his unique status: the Only Begotten.

It is an unusual term for modern speakers. We do not often speak of "begetting," and we know the word "begat," perhaps, only from the long genealogies as they are rendered in old translations of the Old Testament. Nevertheless, every Sunday and ever since the fourth century, Christians have professed their belief in Christ as the "Only Begotten Son of God." We even sing the term—though it is not particularly musical—in the ancient hymn we call the "Gloria": "Lord Jesus Christ, Only Begotten Son, Lord God, Lamb of God, Son of the Father." What do we mean by this mysterious term?

A little bit of historical background can help us to understand what God is revealing. The terms "only begotten" and "only begotten Son" are equivalent English translations of the same Greek word: *monogenes*. Though the term is unusual to us, it had a quite ordinary meaning to people in the ancient world. It is a compound word, made up of *mono*, meaning "only," and *gennesis*, meaning "beginning," "birth," or "origin." The Gospels apply *monogenes* to a parent's sole child, as in the case of the widow's son in Luke 7:12; the only daughter of the synagogue's ruler in Luke 8:42; and the only son of a pleading father in Luke 9:38.

The term "only begotten" conveys two things: uniqueness and origin.

Jesus is the *Only* Begotten. He is unique. Only the divine Word is eternally Son in relation to the eternal Father. Their relation is outside time; it is before the beginning. The Father has always been fathering the Son, eternally. This relationship is unique and quite unlike human begetting, which takes place in a sequence of events over the course of time. A human father must precede his son. My father was born in 1909, and in the usual turn of events, I was born later, in 1940. The divine Persons of the Trinity, however, are coeternal. They coexist outside time, and there has never been a moment when one has been without the others.

Thus, the term "only begotten" can illuminate God's life for us, but it also challenges us to think beyond ordinary human categories. This is how revelation works. God accommodates himself to us by using our language and even taking on our nature, but he also calls upon us to reach upward to him, to the *super*natural, as he makes us his children and shares his divine nature.

The Firstborn of Creation

We find the same dynamic at work in the Scripture passage at the beginning of this chapter from the Letter to the Colossians. In his famous hymn to Christ's preexistence, St. Paul refers to the Son as "the firstborn of all creation" (1:15). It is a phrase that can give (and has given) rise to confusion. Some of it is simply the same problem we have when we consider the term "only begotten." We think of it in terms of human reproduction and the earthly experience of time, but now the new term adds a new difficulty. To modern readers, "firstborn" implies not only a father preceding a son, but also other children arriving afterward.

This implication simply does not exist in the original language of Scripture. "Firstborn" was a legal term for the heir who had a right to inherit the family's estate. The father traditionally passed whatever legacy he had to his eldest son. As the "Only Begotten," Christ possesses all creation as his birthright. Whatever the Father has is the Son's forever, since both Father and Son are immortal, without beginning or end.

In his Letter to the Romans, St. Paul does indeed refer to Jesus as "the firstborn among many brothers" (8:29). Even so, Christ remains the "Only Begotten." He alone is the One who possesses divine sonship by nature. He alone is begotten by the Father and "born of the Father before all ages." Through baptism he now has many brothers and sisters, but this is because he has shared his life and nature with us. What he has by nature, he has given us by grace.

As we recite the Creed, God wants us to think and speak not in natural, earthly physical terms. God wants us to think and speak primarily in terms of the spiritual, supernatural, and heavenly life he has given us. In Christ the eternal Son, we are God's children who share the everlasting inheritance of the eternal Word.

Jesus the Only Begotten possesses a glory that is unique (John 1:14), and so he is uniquely able to reveal the Father to us (1:18). Nothing so demonstrates that "God is love" as the fact that "he gave his only Son" for the sake of our salvation (1 John 4:8; John 3:16). We may even say that our salvation hinges on our profession of belief in Jesus as the Only Begotten: "Whoever believes in him will not be condemned, but whoever does not believe has already been condemned, because he has not believed in the name of the only Son of God" (John 3:18). So when we recite the Creed, it is no small matter!

The Letter to the Colossians also refers to Christ as "the image of the invisible God" (1:15), and this, too, is a unique title. The Book of Genesis tells us that "in the beginning," God created man and woman in the divine image (1:1, 27). But Christ's generation from the Father is essentially different from our human origins. We have been created in God's image, but Christ alone *is* that image; and, as the Only Begotten, he is the image of the Father from all eternity.

Long ago, in the fourth century, there was a priest named Arius who was confused about Jesus' identity. He read the same Scriptures you and I have read in the course of this chapter, but he concluded that the tradition from the apostles must be wrong. He reasoned in a grossly natural way that if God is Jesus' Father, he must have preceded Jesus in time. Thus, according to Arius, only "the Father" was true God, and Jesus was merely the first creature. Arius had a slogan: "There was when he was not." There was a time when the Word did not exist.

The Church rejected Arius's idea as heresy, as a deadly poison. To deny the eternity of the Son is to deny that God is eternally Father. To deny the apostolic doctrine of the Trinity is to deny that God is love. Arius thought he was making Christianity more reasonable, but he was really making it unbearable.

Neither Jesus nor the Spirit has an origin in time. The three divine Persons are coeternal. When we speak of Jesus as "Only Begotten" and "born of the Father before all ages," we are not talking about a temporal sequence of events, but rather about a relationship of love.

Yet we enter that relationship ourselves in a temporal way. We do so by means of the sacraments. Pope Benedict said of Jesus: "He is the food that gives eternal life, because he is the

Only-Begotten Son of God who is in the Father's heart, who came to give man life in fullness, to introduce man into the very life of God."[9]

How can this truth transform me?

We desire salvation. We want the final word about ourselves to be something other than sin and death, which is all that fallen nature seems to hold out for us.

The salvation Christ offers us is so much more than that. It is far more, in fact, than we could ever hope for. We wish for a reprieve from death. Christ gives not merely immortality, but a share of eternal life. He gives us not just glorified humanity, which he himself has enjoyed since the resurrection; he gives us a share of his divinity.

If he were not Only Begotten, as we profess that he is, he would not have his divinity to share with us. Salvation is so much more than we allow ourselves to think it is. When we recite the Creed, we are retraining our mind for the sweet task of contemplating the gift of eternal life that we have received as adopted children of God.

How do I live it?

The saints often counsel us with the Latin phrase *Memento mori*, which means "Remember you must die." Some people say this is morbid, but it is not. It is good for us, now and then, to consider the fact that God has made death to be the portal to a far more glorious life. If we are faithful, if we live up to our profession of faith, we shall know the life that Christ has known from all eternity.

The funeral liturgy reprises so many of the symbols of the Sacrament of Baptism: the casket is sprinkled with water and clothed in a white garment. At our baptism we began life as children of God, because our lives at that moment were united to the Only Begotten. At death we bring true life not to its end, but to its completion, its fullness.

We should think, now and then, on these two stations of our earthly life—baptism and death. As we pray, we can ask the Lord to fill us with a spirit of joy and gratitude for all that he has done for us—and will do—if we stay faithful to him.

How do I share it with others?

People need friends, and it can be heartening for them to know that Jesus is their friend, but they must also know who Jesus really is. Earthly friends will let us down. Jesus never will, because he is God.

We all thrive when we experience parental love. We are created with this need. Yet no earthly parent is perfect, and some are even abusive and neglectful of their children. We should help those who have endured family difficulties to come to a deeper understanding of *life in Christ*. In the eternal Son, we enjoy the love of the eternal Father even now on earth, and we look forward to knowing it far more perfectly in heaven. This can be a great comfort and consolation for people.

You may sometimes encounter neighbors or co-workers who mock Christianity based on an overly natural reading of the Scriptures. They are like Nicodemus, who asked Jesus how a grown man could possibly be born again (John 3:4). We should patiently try to help such people see the supernatural and spiritual sense of the words of Scripture. It may take some time. This was one of St. Augustine's great obstacles on his way to conversion. But he overcame it, with help from Christian friends, and became one of the greatest saints in the history of the Church. Nicodemus, too, overcame his difficulties and stood by Jesus courageously (John 7:50-51; 19:39).

Questions for reflection and discussion

1. It can be difficult to imagine existence outside of time and space. Why do you think it is important to think about Jesus as coeternal with the Father and the Spirit? How does that deepen your understanding of who he is? How does it affect your relationship with him?

2. What obstacles do you face in thinking about the spiritual, supernatural, and heavenly life that God has given you? How might Scripture help you grasp the essence of this life? How might more time spent in prayer and conversation with Jesus help?

3. What kind of thinking led Arius to make the wrong conclusion about the nature of the Trinity? How can we guard against such thinking in our own lives?

4. How often do you think about death? Does it scare you? What assurances can you seek from Scripture and Church tradition that death is a portal to a far more glorious life? How might the reading of the lives of the saints, especially the martyrs, strengthen your faith?

5. How have other Christians helped you understand your faith in a deeper way? What might you say or do to help your friends and family better understand the gift of eternal life?

Looking for more?

▶ See the *Catechism of the Catholic Church*, 240–241, 430–455, and 1701.

▶ See the *United States Catholic Catechism for Adults*, chapter 7, "The Good News: God Has Sent His Son."

▶ In the Scriptures, see Mark 1:10-11.

Chapter 3

Jesus Christ: Doctrine and Identity

> *God from God, Light from Light,*
> *true God from true God,*
> *begotten, not made, consubstantial with*
>   *the Father;*
> *through him all things were made.*

What is the revelation?

When Jesus went into the region of Caesarea Philippi he asked his disciples, "Who do people say that the Son of Man is?" They replied, "Some say John the Baptist, others Elijah, still others Jeremiah or one of the prophets." He said to them, "But who do you say that I am?" Simon Peter said in reply, "You are the Messiah, the Son of the living God." Jesus said to him in reply, "Blessed are you, Simon son of Jonah. For flesh and blood has not revealed this to you, but my heavenly Father. And so I say to you, you are Peter, and upon this rock I will build my church."

—The Gospel According to St. Matthew 16:13-18

What does it mean?

Some people claim that Jesus was indifferent to doctrine. They like to imagine him as a man who went about practicing random acts of kindness without a care for what people believed. Doctrine, they say, came much later, from the Church, and its worries did not reflect the mind of Jesus.

But we see in Jesus' exchange with Simon Peter that this is simply not true. He was, in fact, intensely concerned about doctrine. The question he asked his disciples was the most fundamental question of Christian faith: who is Jesus?

The apostles responded by listing a variety of answers they had heard from their contemporaries. Some said he was a prophet, others a teacher or a preacher of morals. So we see that in Jesus' own lifetime, there were profound differences of opinion about his identity. People who knew him personally, who had seen him heal and had heard him preach, still fundamentally misunderstood him. Each one of them had a cherished version of "my Jesus," a figment of their imagination. But their version of Jesus was not true; it was not real. At best, it was incomplete, and so it could not save.

The real Jesus refused to be defined by mere human opinions ("flesh and blood," as he says in Matthew 13:17). His identity came not from opinion polls, democratic process, or the fond wishes of genial people. His identity as the Son of God was eternal and true—and now it was being revealed by the Father to a particular person, Peter, who would from that moment be the rock foundation of the Church. If the Church is concerned about doctrine, it is because Jesus made it that way.

He wanted his disciples to get it right, because to get it wrong is to worship the wrong god.

Doctrine is key to identity—and not just Jesus' identity, but our own as well. What we believe about Jesus sets us apart, defines us. To be Catholic means something specific. It means to hold certain doctrines as true and to reject others as false, just as the apostles did, just as Jesus did. It means to stand freely on the side of the martyrs, and not as a slave to the dominant culture, the reigning government, or the latest fashions. It means to love not only "my Jesus," but the Jesus who really lived, who still lives, and who truly saves.

The first Christians knew Jesus as every subsequent generation of Catholics have known Jesus: through the Scriptures he inspired and the Church he founded. These are not two ways, but one; and so there cannot be "my Jesus" and "their Jesus." As we read in the Letter to the Hebrews, "Jesus Christ is the same yesterday, today, and forever. Do not be carried away by all kinds of strange teaching" (13:8-9). Jesus protected us from strange teaching when he breathed on the Church at Pentecost. The gift of the Holy Spirit was given to his Church so that the Church would always preach the true Jesus.

An Act of Faith

Jesus' question is always timely, always in season, always directed to each of us, and it calls forth acts of faith. The doubting apostle, Thomas, was professing faith in basic doctrinal terms when he cried out, "My Lord and my God!" (John 20:28).

The Creed is the Church's perennial response to Jesus' question. He asks each of us, "Who do you say that I am?" and each of us responds, "I believe . . . " And we state our beliefs in very specific doctrinal terms—as Peter did, as Thomas did—because, like the apostles, we live in a time when there is a great and widespread temptation to make Jesus something less than he is—to portray him as *merely* a teacher, *just* an agitator, or *simply* a wonderworker and healer.

Jesus may have filled all those roles, but we cannot reduce him to any one of them, or even the lot of them together. To do so would be untrue to Jesus' life. For he is "God from God, Light from Light, true God from true God, begotten, not made, consubstantial with the Father; through him all things were made."

In Jesus' own age and in every age since then, there have been people who judged such claims to be extreme. They are embarrassed by what they see as excess or exaggeration. But as we have seen, it is Jesus himself who has revealed his divine nature to us. He showed himself to be God, and God must stand alone at the extreme end of any chain of being, any scale of goodness, any range of holiness.

People in every age will face the temptation to make Jesus fit contemporary categories of what is "rational" or "scientific." Yet their own ideas of rationality will soon prove to be passing fads, while the doctrine of Christ endures.

Jesus knew his claims would scandalize people and seem too good to be true. That is why he said, "Whoever is ashamed of me and of my words, the Son of Man will be ashamed of when he comes in his glory and in the glory of the Father" (Luke 9:26). St. Paul, too, had occasion to say to the Romans, "I am not ashamed of the gospel. It is the power of God for the salvation of everyone who believes" (1:16).

Doctrine can also fall victim to a sort of reverse snobbery. There was a trend some decades ago toward minimizing doctrinal content in religion textbooks. Students would encounter Jesus as friend, confidant, counselor, teacher, helper, and so forth, but they would not have to grapple with terms like "God from God . . . begotten, not made, consubstantial with the Father." Eventually, so the theory went, they would reason their way from their personal experiences to Jesus' divinity.

The problem is that even in the most brilliant minds, reason is limited. Even geniuses make big mistakes. If reason alone could lead us to sure knowledge of God, we would not have needed a revelation. Arius was a brilliant man, but he reasoned his way to very wrong conclusions about Jesus.

It is sad to realize that many young people walked away from religious education with only vague ideas about Jesus—that he was a good teacher and a nice guy.

In the Creed and in the Scriptures, the Church speaks of Jesus with words that are bold indeed, words that express faith and words that demand faith. In the Eastern churches, he is worshipped as *Pantokrator*—"the Almighty, the All-Powerful"—a term found in the Book of Revelation and St. Paul's Second Letter to the Corinthians. We call upon him as the Alpha and Omega, "the beginning and end" of everything. Yet he himself has no beginning and end. Through him all things were made, and he rules all creation as sovereign "King of kings" (1 Timothy 6:15; Revelation 19:16). He rules creation because he transcends it; he is uncreated, "begotten, not made."

Jesus is *consubstantial* with the Father, and that is why we trust his revelation. Only God can reveal the true God to us (John 14:8-11). That word, "consubstantial," is the great contribution of the Council of Nicaea in A.D. 325. The bishops hesitated to use it because it does not appear in Scripture, but they concluded that it was the only word capable of describing Jesus' relationship with the Father as that relationship appears in Scripture. Father and Son are of the same substance. They share a single divine nature.

What should be most remarkable to us is that this *Pantokrator*—the Almighty, the All-Powerful, true God from true God—also wants to be our friend, confidant, counselor, helper, and teacher! We lose nothing when we gain doctrine. We are so much the richer for knowing *more* of the truth that Christ has revealed.

Jesus questions his disciples—and he questions us—in insistently doctrinal terms: "Who do *you* say that I am?"

How can this truth transform me?

Prayerful study is an indispensable part of any adult faith. God has revealed heavenly mysteries to us, and he has given us the grace to *want* to know the mysteries, but he will not force us to draw near to them and study them. God wants us freely to correspond to his grace.

At least half of any communication is listening. That's as true in our relationship with God as in any human friendship or family bond. Our prayer should be more than just asking God for good things. We should also be asking for a greater knowledge of who he is.

When we know that Jesus Christ is "God from God, Light from Light, true God from true God," we will see his light and see all things in his light. This is a grace we can ask for and receive. Like any grace, it will change us. That's because our eyes will be opened. We will recognize his presence in ourselves, in others, and in the sacraments of the Church, especially in the Eucharist. How differently we would live our lives if we saw Christ's light all the time!

How do I live it?

We would fail at friendship if we showed no curiosity whatsoever about our friends' personal lives—if we never asked them about their background, family, children, siblings, schooling, work, or goals in life. If we do not show at least as much desire to know Jesus Christ, can we truly call our relationship a "friendship"? Can we honestly call it "loving"?

Jesus has told us so much about who he is and what he values, about his Father and his heavenly home, about his banquet and his future plans. It remains for us to listen. We listen when we make time to pray every day. We must be disciplined about it, because we know it is important. Our relationship with Christ cannot grow if we do not spend time with him in conversation.

We should also take up a disciplined study of the *Catechism of the Catholic Church*. Another equally good source is the *United States Catholic Catechism for Adults*, which is faithful to the teaching of the *Catechism* and presents it in a highly readable format. The heart of the *Catechism* is a detailed exposition of the doctrine of Jesus Christ. It can be helpful to examine our preconceptions about him in the light of Church teaching. We want to be right about the doctrine of Jesus Christ, because we know that doctrine is important to him. We, like St. Peter, want to hear Jesus say, "Blessed are you! . . . For flesh and blood has not revealed this to you, but my heavenly Father" (Matthew 16:17).

How do I share it with others?

Healthy friendship is expansive, not exclusive. We want all our friends to know the joy of our companionship with a new friend. If we are friends of Jesus, we will want to share Jesus' company with the whole world, and we will want the world to know Christ deeply.

Earlier, we spoke of the anemic quality of some religious education in the past. If we ourselves suffer from the effects of this, we don't have to abandon ourselves to ignorance. Neither do we have to sit back and allow others to remain in ignorance. As friends of Jesus, we have a deep obligation to help others encounter Christ *as he wishes to be encountered*—and that includes doctrine. "Go, therefore, and make disciples of all nations, . . . teaching them" (Matthew 28:19, 20).

What can you do to share doctrine more effectively and make up for what was lacking in past generations? Can you teach in your parish's religious education program? Help with RCIA? Offer a class in a nearby prison or juvenile detention center? Will you write letters to the editor when you find misunderstandings about Christianity in the media? Look for opportunities to spread good doctrine. Ask Jesus to show you where your contribution is most needed.

Questions for reflection and discussion

1. Why do you think that Jesus asked the apostles, "Who do you say that I am?" Why was it important that they understand his true identity? Why is it important for all disciples of Jesus to understand this truth?

2. "Jesus Christ is the same yesterday, today, and forever" (Hebrews 13:8). What does this mean to you? In what ways does this Scripture verse demonstrate that doctrine must be based on divine revelation, not on human opinion?

3. Have there been times in your life when your knowledge of Jesus increased significantly? What were the circumstances? How might you be able to take another step today in increasing your knowledge about our Lord?

4. How much time do you spend in prayer just listening to God? What are some difficulties you face in doing so? How might you get to know Jesus better if you talked less and listened more?

5. If someone asked you, "Who is Jesus?" how would you respond? What would be the most important things for you to share with them?

Looking for more?

▶ See the *Catechism of the Catholic Church*, 50–53, 65, 94, 249–252.

▶ See the *United States Catholic Catechism for Adults*, chapter 7, "The Good News: God Has Sent His Son."

▶ In the Scriptures, see John 1:3-5, 9-13 and 1 John 1:5-7; 2:20-23.

▶ See *The Gift of Blessed John Paul II: A Celebration of His Enduring Legacy*, chapter 1, "Focus on the Future: *Redemptor Hominis* (The Redeemer of Man)."[10]

Chapter 4

The Incarnation

> *For us men and for our salvation*
> *he came down from heaven,*
> *and by the Holy Spirit was incarnate of the*
> *   Virgin Mary,*
> *and became man.*

What is the revelation?

What was from the beginning,
what we have heard,
what we have seen with our eyes,
what we looked upon
and touched with our hands
concerns the Word of life—
   for the life was made visible;
we have seen it and testify to it
and proclaim to you the eternal life
that was with the Father and was made visible to us—
   what we have seen and heard
we proclaim now to you,
so that you too may have fellowship with us;

for our fellowship is with the Father
and with his Son, Jesus Christ.
We are writing this so that our joy may be complete.

—First Letter of St. John 1:1-4

What does it mean?

Theologians sometimes joke that original sin is the only empirically verifiable doctrine of the Christian faith. Everything else requires some measure of trust on our part. But we see the effects of original sin all the time—in suffering and death, but also in human selfishness, cruelty, and exploitation.

The *Catechism of the Catholic Church* refers to original sin in a memorable way as the "reverse side" of the gospel (389). Jesus came to save; he is our Savior. That is indeed good news! But he came precisely because we needed saving. Humanity could not remove itself from the mire and tangle of sin, which began with the disobedience of our first parents. As the *Catechism* explains:

Although it is proper to each individual (cf. Council of Trent: DS 1513), original sin does not have the character of a personal fault in any of Adam's descendants. It is a deprivation of original holiness and justice, but human nature has not been totally corrupted: it is wounded in the natural powers proper to it; subject to ignorance, suffering, and the dominion of death; and inclined to sin—an inclination to evil that is called "concupiscence." Baptism, by imparting the life of Christ's grace, erases original sin and turns a man back towards God, but the consequences for nature, weakened and inclined to evil, persist in man and summon him to spiritual battle. (CCC 405)

Although we are not to blame, the *fault* is ours because we have inherited it. It is as if we own a family business that the previous generation very badly mismanaged. We are left with the mess and an unbearable burden of debt.

If there's one doctrine life teaches us in an empirically verifiable way, it is that we need someone to come from outside the mess of our history and save us.

Such is the human story as told by the prophets of the Old Testament. It is a drama that unfolds in one sin after another, with one human figure after another appearing to bring a partial rescue, a partial redemption—yet always foreshadowing something greater. At the very moment after Adam and Eve had committed the original sin, God promised that Eve's "offspring" would arise to oppose and vanquish the power of evil in the world (Genesis 3:15).

God promised that he would send a Messiah. He would send a savior, a redeemer, someone to put it all back together again, and that was the hope held out by Israel's prophets. They talked about restoration and healing, and they spoke of it in lavish terms. The age of the Messiah would be like a banquet. It would be a time of peace and prosperity. Eventually came the last of the prophets, St. John the Baptist, who proclaimed that Jesus of Nazareth is that long-awaited Messiah.

The marvel of God's plan is that it gave us so much more than we could have hoped for. Jesus is the eternal "Word became flesh"—Christ came from outside our history—yet he "made his dwelling among us" (John 1:14). He came from heaven, yet he emerged within our history as the offspring of a woman. "He came down from heaven, and by the Holy Spirit was incarnate of the Virgin Mary, and became man." This is the mystery of the *Incarnation*, which we profess in the Creed. "Incarnate" means simply "enfleshed," derived from the Latin for God's coming in human flesh.

Why did he do this? For us and for our salvation!

The "Marvelous Exchange"

The liturgy refers to the Incarnation as the "marvelous exchange." The Son of God became the Son of Man so that we could become children of God. He took on our pain to give us a share of his life, a share of his eternal sonship. St. Augustine said, "In [Christ] the divinity of the Only Begotten One was made to share in our mortality, that we might share in his immortality."[11]

We are given a share in what we could never have by nature, what we could never have by right. This is possible only because we hold fast to Christ's uniqueness. What he has by nature, we have by grace. What he has enjoyed from all eternity, he gives to us as a gift.

Our part is to accept it by making our act of faith, as we do in the Creed.

Remember Peter's response when Jesus asked, "Who do you say I am?" We make the same response, and it is only by grace that we can do so. The faith is a grace, and our response—*our* faith—is also a gift. "Flesh and blood has not revealed this to you," Jesus said, "but my heavenly Father" (Matthew 16:17).

The whole New Testament, the whole gospel narrative, is told in order to draw from us an act of faith in Jesus, the incarnate Word—true God, as we have seen, but true man as well. St. Paul, in his Letter to the Philippians (2:6-11), puts this in very poetic terms, beginning with the Son in heaven, but tracing his dramatic movement to earth:

> Though he was in the form of God,
> [he] did not regard equality with God
>   something to be grasped.
>   Rather, he emptied himself,
> taking the form of a slave,
> coming in human likeness;
> and found human in appearance,
>   he humbled himself,
> becoming obedient to death,
>   even death on a cross.
> Because of this, God greatly exalted him
> and bestowed on him the name
> that is above every name,
>   that at the name of Jesus
> every knee should bend,
> of those in heaven and on earth and under the earth,
>   and every tongue confess that
> Jesus Christ is Lord,
> to the glory of God the Father.

Paul speaks of Jesus quite plainly as God. He gives him divine titles such as "Lord" and gives Jesus the "glory" (Philippians 2:11) and worship that is due only to God. He calls upon not only human beings but angels as well to bend the knee at the very mention of Jesus' name (2:10).

St. Paul's first hearers understood the profound significance of this proclamation—and so must we. It is the heart and soul of our Catholic faith. It is what the Creed is all about: God became man in order to reveal the life of the Trinity and share the life of the Trinity.

Why would God come among us? And furthermore, why would God come among us as an obscure wandering rabbi from the backwater of Nazareth? And what does it mean?

It means that God chose to restore us through *our very participation* in the act of restoration. It was in Adam that we sinned. It was in our human nature that we failed; and God, in love, chose that we should participate in the repair. You and I, through the grace of God, can participate in our own salvation. In Christ, our nature, the human nature shared by every single person on this planet, is involved in our redemption. The eternal Word—"God from God, Light from Light, true God from true God," spiritual, infinite, majestic, one with God—has taken up our frail, finite, fumbling human nature. And that is what the Incarnation is all about.

That is what we believe. That is what the Creed professes. The celebration of the Incarnation is the recognition that God chose to be one with us so that we could be one with him. Whatever, then, happened to Jesus—whatever he freely, lovingly, willingly accepted in his human life—would be transformed. He took on suffering and death, the dreadful things in human existence, and he made them the very means of salvation. He showed us how we, too, could participate in salvation by means of our suffering and even our death. St. Paul's faith was so strong that he could not help but "rejoice" in his sufferings: "Now I rejoice in my sufferings for your sake, and in my flesh I am filling up what is lacking in the afflictions of Christ on behalf of his body, which is the church" (Colossians 1:24).

Through the Incarnation, God has given us the power to play a role in the drama of salvation. Our suffering is not futile. It's not for nothing. When it is united to "the afflictions of Christ," it is offered for the sake of love.

It seems almost too good to be true, and in the first generation of Christianity, there were people who claimed to be Christian but refused to believe in the Incarnation. The apostles themselves at first found this teaching hard to believe. However, belief in the Incarnation is what makes our faith specifically Christian. "This is how you can know the Spirit of God," St. John wrote. "Every spirit that acknowledges Jesus Christ *come in the flesh* belongs to God, and every spirit that does not acknowledge Jesus does not belong to God. This is the spirit of antichrist that, as you heard, is to come, but in fact is already in the world" (1 John 4:2-3, emphasis added).

The bishops of the Church stated this doctrine with increasing precision through the early councils. We have already mentioned Nicaea (A.D. 325). Other councils that dealt with this mystery were Constantinople (381), Ephesus (431), and Chalcedon (451). The correct understanding of the Incarnation was the first order of doctrinal business for the Church. The bishops addressed this matter long before they took up such questions as, for example, the accepted canon (the list of books) of the Scriptures.

A Living Faith

What took place from the days of the apostolic Church down to the Council of Nicaea might be described as a gradual, unspecified clarification of the implications dependent on the Church's faith proclamation. The process began with the faith as something given, which is to be reverenced and understood insofar as reason can penetrate the mystery of God's revelation. The process moves from what is given to what is implied. The affirmation of further statements about the faith enables the living faith to develop. It flourishes yet does not change. It grows but is not altered.

Jesus is true God through the divine nature he received from his divine Father. But he is true man from the human nature he received from his Blessed Mother. The two natures belong to just one person. And it has always been impossible for Christians to tell the story of redemption apart from the Blessed Virgin Mary's cooperation. St. Paul summed it up: "But when the fullness of time had come, God sent his Son, born of a woman, born under the law, to ransom those under the law, so that we might receive adoption" (Galatians 4:4-5). Mary is the way Christ came to us. From her own substance, she gave the Word his human flesh. Her cooperation with grace set the standard for our obedience.

Our downfall was the sin of Adam and Eve. Our salvation came by way of Christ, who is the New Adam (Romans 5:12-

19). The Church Fathers, as early as the middle of the second century, saw that the Blessed Virgin Mary cooperated in salvation as Eve had cooperated in sin. They hailed Mary as the "New Eve." We hail Mary still today, as the Church has ever done, in our popular devotions and liturgical feasts. She is not divine; she is merely human, but purely human in a way unsullied by original sin. She is a beautiful and essential part of the redemption her Son has won for us. He has made us brothers and sisters because he is the "firstborn" of all of us (Colossians 1:15). Because we are saved, his Father is "Our Father" (Matthew 6:9). His mother is our mother. That is the essence of Catholic devotion to Mary.

We could not have extricated ourselves from the mess of sin and death. Nor can we do it today. The latest greatest technology cannot help us, and it never will. We need God—specifically, we need God who became man—for us and for our salvation.

How can this truth transform me?

The Word became flesh. The more you meditate on this astounding truth, the more it will dazzle you, just as it has dazzled artists, musicians, writers, and countless others for more than two thousand years. God has come down from the inaccessible heavens to meet you—personally. In everything you do, then, stretch forward to meet him in gratitude and joy. Jesus, God-made-man, has brought you salvation!

How do I live it?

To live the doctrine of the Incarnation is simply to be a Christian. To live it better is to become a better Christian. As Pope Blessed John Paul used to tell his congregations, "Become who you are!" In the Incarnation, Christ took on our human nature, so this mystery touches on every aspect of our life of faith—and every aspect of your life and mine.

It is Christ we are becoming. So it helps if we know Christ, whose life we have come to share in baptism. He is our deepest identity. We should get to know him well, and the Church has a ready-made program for this purpose. If we go to Mass on Sundays and holy days, we are living the mysteries of Jesus' life. At Christmas we celebrate his birth. A little later, we mark his appearance to the wise men, then his baptism in the Jordan, then his passion, death, resurrection, and ascension. In the course of every year, we trace the outline of his life. We hear it proclaimed in the readings. We consume it as grace in the sacraments. We make it more deeply our own.

By living on earth, Jesus showed us how a human life should be lived. This should be the standard by which we approach morality. Some years back, it was trendy to ask, "What would Jesus do?" Young people had "WWJD" imprinted on rings, bracelets, and other paraphernalia. Though the trend has played itself out, the question remains a good one for us to ask ourselves. In fact, long before it was trendy, the sisters taught us to use questions like that one whenever we faced a difficult decision.

How do I share it with others?

Help others to see that everything in the world has changed because of Jesus Christ—not simply in a visible way, but in its very meaning. It is true that no other person has ever had such an impact on history. In that sense, we continue to see the influence and work of Jesus in countless acts of charity, great and small, in billions of lives. But the greatest difference is interior and invisible. Jesus' life and death have given profound meaning, dignity, and even power to every human life and death.

How can you *not* let others know about this? Without it, they're impoverished. And yet even some Catholics seem to lack a sufficiently deep knowledge of the transforming power of the doctrine.

Join a Bible study—or start one. You can do this in your parish or your home. Find a good Catholic program, and let it take you and your brothers and sisters in Christ prayerfully through the Scriptures. Jesus' public life is an image in time of his eternal life in heaven. We call the events of his life "mysteries" for that reason—they point beyond themselves to something that's hidden in God. The more we study and internalize these mysteries, the better able we are to share them with others.

Pray the Rosary, and invite others to pray it with you. It is a powerful way to meditate on the mysteries of Jesus' life, accompanied by his mother and our mother.

Spend time in conversation with Jesus. He's not just a historical figure you're learning about. He's not George Washington or Abraham Lincoln. He is God become man; he is alive, and he loves you.

There is no limit to what you can do to live a fuller life in Christ and to share that life with others. This is a topic as vast as the Church and as varied as the lives of the saints. Get active in your parish. Ask your pastor to help you discern your special gifts for service. Read the lives of the saints. See what the Incarnation has made possible for you.

Questions for reflection and discussion

1. Why is it important to acknowledge the effects of original sin in the world and in our own lives? What are the risks if we fail to acknowledge them?

2. By becoming human, Jesus showed us how to live. What events in Jesus' life have been most helpful to you when you face crises, moral dilemmas, or major decisions in your own life? How do these events give you clarity?

3. Have you ever, like St. Paul, "rejoiced" in your sufferings (Colossians 1:24) by offering them for the sake of love? How can the knowledge of Christ's suffering help you in your own trials?

4. Mary is Jesus' mother and our mother too. In what ways does she help us to understand the mystery of the Incarnation? What does she teach us about cooperating with God's grace?

5. Reread the Scripture passage at the beginning of this chapter. In its light, consider these questions: Why does the Catholic Church encourage the use of sacramentals in devotion, such as sacred images, holy water, or rosary beads? How does this relate to the doctrine of the Incarnation?

Looking for more?

▶ On the doctrine of the Lord's Incarnation, see the *Catechism of the Catholic Church*, 461, 464, and the *United States Catholic Catechism for Adults*, chapter 7, "The Good News: God Has Sent His Son."

▶ On the "marvelous exchange," see 2 Corinthians 8:9; Galatians 4:4-6; Romans 8:14-17, 29; 1 John 3:1-2; 2 Peter 1:4.

▶ On original sin, see the *Catechism of the Catholic Church*, 389, 396–412, and the *United States Catholic Catechism for Adults*, chapter 6, "Man and Woman in the Beginning."

▶ On the true celebration of the Incarnation at Christmas, see Pope Benedict XVI, General Audience, December 21, 2011.[12]

▶ See *The Gift of Blessed John Paul II: A Celebration of His Enduring Legacy*, chapter 9, "Behold Your Mother: *Redemptoris Mater* (The Mother of the Redeemer)."

Chapter 5

Jesus' Passion, Death, and Resurrection

> For our sake he was crucified under
> Pontius Pilate,
> he suffered death and was buried,
> and rose again on the third day
> in accordance with the Scriptures.

What is the revelation?

Now the feast of Unleavened Bread, called the Passover, was drawing near, and the chief priests and the scribes were seeking a way to put him to death, for they were afraid of the people. Then Satan entered into Judas, the one surnamed Iscariot, who was counted among the Twelve, and he went to the chief priests and temple guards to discuss a plan for handing him over to them. They were pleased and agreed to pay him money. He accepted their offer and sought a favorable opportunity to hand him over to them in the absence of a crowd.

When the day of the Feast of Unleavened Bread arrived, the day for sacrificing the Passover lamb, he sent out Peter and John, instructing them, "Go and make preparations for us to eat the Passover." They asked him, "Where do you want us to make the preparations?" And he answered them, "When you go into the city, a man will meet you carrying a jar of water. Follow him into the house that he enters and say to the master of the house, 'The teacher says to you, "Where is the guest room where I may eat the Passover with my disciples?"'" He will show you a large upper room that is furnished. Make the preparations there." Then they went off and found everything exactly as he had told them, and there they prepared the Passover.

When the hour came, he took his place at table with the apostles. He said to them, "I have eagerly desired to eat this Passover with you before I suffer, for, I tell you, I shall not eat it [again] until there is fulfillment in the kingdom of God." Then he took a cup, gave thanks, and said, "Take this and share it among yourselves; for I tell you [that] from this time on I shall not drink of the fruit of the vine until the kingdom of God comes." Then he took the bread, said the blessing, broke it, and gave it to them, saying, "This is my body, which will be given for you; do this in memory of me." And likewise the cup after they had eaten, saying, "This cup is the new covenant in my blood, which will be shed for you."

—The Gospel According to St. Luke 22:1-20

What does it mean?

I live in a capital city—my nation's capital—and many of my fellow citizens mark time by presidential administrations. You might hear people say, "I've been working in this shop since the Carter years." Or "I haven't had a parking ticket since the Reagan era."

The Creed does this too. It speaks of Jesus in verifiably historical terms. It places him on a timeline. The most important events of his earthly life, it tells us, took place "under Pontius Pilate," when a certain man served as the Roman Empire's colonial governor in Judea.

The historical references make clear that our profession of faith is quite unlike the religions of ancient Greece, Rome, Egypt, or Babylon. The Creed begins in heaven with God, but it comes to earth with God in the Incarnation of the Word. The Christian revelation takes place not in some mythological era, not "once upon a time," but at a particular moment in history, just like your life and mine.

Notice that the Creed tells us not of Jesus' miracles, or his sermons, or his travels. It tells us of just a few events that took place at the very end of his time on earth.

These events—his suffering, death, burial, and resurrection—are sometimes referred to collectively as the "paschal mystery." That name, too, points to a precise historical moment. We call them "paschal" because the Gospels tell us that these momentous events took place on and around the Jewish feast of *Pesach*, which we call "Passover" in English. The timing was no accident and no coincidence. As we say in the Creed, Jesus' sacred passion took place "in accordance with the Scriptures." Since the dawn of history, God had been setting the stage for the climactic scene in the drama of salvation. It was fitting that Jesus should be crucified "for our sake" on the feast of Passover.

Liberation from Slavery and Death

Passover, after all, was a festival that recalled a saving event from many centuries before. It commemorated the deliverance of God's chosen people from slavery in Egypt. The people of Israel were saved from harsh servitude so that they could live and worship freely in the land God had given to their ancestors, to Abraham and Isaac and Jacob.

Jesus, however, came to bring a far greater liberation—he came to bring salvation. He came to save all people from slavery to sin and death. He came to save us so that we might share eternal life with God in heaven.

In the old Passover, the customary sacrifice was a lamb. In the paschal mystery too, we find the victim identified as the "Lamb of God."

The Passover theme dominates St. Luke's description of Jesus' last meal with his disciples. In the brief passage quoted at the beginning of this chapter, the word "Passover" appears six times. When St. John tells the story of Jesus' crucifixion, he makes sure that we see it in the context of the Passover: "It was preparation day for Passover, and it was about noon," John writes, when Pilate handed Jesus over to be crucified (John 19:14, 16). Noon was the hour when the priests began to slaughter the Passover lambs in the Jerusalem Temple. Here, at the climax of his Gospel, John is bringing to fulfillment the strange oracle of St. John the Baptist that we find in the beginning of his Gospel. There, when John the Baptist first sees Jesus, he cries out, "Behold, the Lamb of God, who takes away the sin of the world!" (1:29).

What a strange title to use for the Messiah. Yet it made perfect sense to the first Christians. St. Paul wrote, "For our paschal lamb, Christ, has been sacrificed" (1 Corinthians 5:7). Jesus came, not only to be with us, but by his death and resurrection to save us and then to remain with us in the Eucharist. This is his mission, his purpose—he came to give his life for our salvation.

In Israel's Passover, there was the offering of the lamb and the shedding of blood for the redemption, the salvation, and the justification of the chosen people. God had brought his people out of bondage into freedom. In the New Testament, Jesus is the Lamb of God. Jesus is the priest who offers the sacrifice of his own body and blood. Jesus' blood washes us and frees us; his flesh feeds us in the new paschal meal he has established: the Holy Mass. And the new paschal meal not only symbolizes his death and resurrection, but it actually makes present the mystery. Every Mass re-presents the saving events that we profess in the Creed.

Jesus' death is the singular, most important moment in all of human history. The paschal mystery is a historical event that happened once, "under Pontius Pilate," but it happened "once for all." The apostles were emphatic about that fact, and it is repeated many times in the New Testament (Hebrews 7:27; 9:12; 9:26; cf. Romans 6:10). "For Christ also died for sins *once for all*, the righteous for the unrighteous, that he might bring us to

God, being put to death in the flesh but made alive in the spirit" (1 Peter 3:18, RSV; emphasis added).

When we pray the traditional devotion known as the Stations of the Cross, we say a prayer that summarizes these truths: "We adore you, O Christ, and we praise you, because by your Holy Cross you have redeemed the world." We pray as we believe, and we believe as we pray: in God's plan Jesus came among us to give his life for our salvation. St. Paul writes in amazement, "Indeed, only with difficulty does one die for a just person, though perhaps for a good person one might even find courage to die. But God proves his love for us in that while we were still sinners Christ died for us" (Romans 5:7-8).

Jesus himself made clear that he acted out of love; he submitted voluntarily. "This is why the Father loves me, because I lay down my life in order to take it up again. No one takes it from me, but I lay it down on my own. I have power to lay it down, and power to take it up again" (John 10:17-18). In his passion as in the Mass—in every aspect of the paschal mystery—Jesus is both priest and victim.

His victimhood is real. His death was as real as our own will be. His friends laid his body in a tomb, and they walked away grieving. But that was not the end of the mystery. On the third day—after his death and burial—Jesus rose again, truly alive and glorified. Jesus returned victorious from the dead, and Easter is the celebration of that event.

Jesus died and Jesus rose. The two events are intimately connected in the Creed, as they are in history.

This is the mystery of the Passover. With Jesus we "pass over" from failure, from death, and from the catastrophic effects of original sin. We pass over to redemption, to grace, to new life.

The paschal mystery is how our salvation came about. It is how our salvation still comes about, as it is re-presented in every Mass. Salvation is not something we deserve; it is not something we could ever earn. But it is something we need, and it arrives as a gift from God who has taken human flesh for this very purpose: "for our sake he was crucified." For our sake he rose again from the dead. We cannot be fulfilled without this salvation. We cannot know true peace apart from it.

God gives it freely, and we must freely take it up. Salvation does not happen apart from our response of faith; it does not happen apart from our belief.

How can this truth transform me?

The truth of the paschal mystery transforms us through the power of the sacraments. Through the sacraments we come to share in Christ's life, and this sharing is very real. So close is our communion with Jesus—when we are baptized, when we are reconciled, when we receive the Holy Eucharist—so close is our communion that we die with him and rise with him!

St. Paul delighted in this fact. His participation in the paschal mystery was not theoretical or symbolic; it was real. "I have been crucified with Christ," he wrote to the Galatians; "yet I live, no longer I, but Christ lives in me; insofar as I now live in the flesh, I live by faith in the Son of God who has loved me and given himself up for me" (2:19-20). "If, then, we have died with Christ, we believe that we shall also live with him" (Romans

6:8). This gives meaning to our suffering, because through the paschal mystery, we become "heirs of God and joint heirs with Christ, if only we suffer with him so that we may also be glorified with him" (Romans 8:17).

All this leads us to desire conversion. We want all of our lives to be lived in the truth of our salvation in the paschal mystery. We want all of our lives to "pass over" into true life. "If then you were raised with Christ, seek what is above, where Christ is seated at the right hand of God. Think of what is above, not of what is on earth. For you have died, and your life is hidden with Christ in God. When Christ your life appears, then you too will appear with him in glory" (Colossians 3:1-4).

How do I live it?

Because of Jesus' death and resurrection, we have the pledge of everlasting life. How does that play out in our lives? It means that we live in hope of rising with Christ. Our lives should be guided by the hope of the resurrection. We direct all our affairs and actions according to the understanding that we already have this new life within us, the Spirit of the risen Lord. We should be living and acting and behaving as Christians by living and acting and behaving as Christ.

Our Easter faith also plays out in the way we deal with death. If we firmly believe in the Creed, if we place our faith in Jesus, if we truly believe that he died and rose and that we will have everlasting life, then we reverence the body of someone who has fallen asleep in the Lord—someone who has died.

In our Mass of Christian Burial, we bring to the church the bodily remains of a Christian who has died, someone who was baptized into the death and resurrection of Jesus, someone who shared our sacraments and our profession of faith. We gather to bury our dead in the hope of the resurrection. We take their remains to holy ground—ground that has been blessed—and we bury them as the friends of Christ buried his body. We live on in Easter hope.

How do I share it with others?

Mortality is a universal fact. It's something we all must face as we grow older and begin to lose friends and family members. Grieving is an inevitable part of living. As people confront the end of earthly life, they tend to be more open to conversations that are spiritual in nature. They are looking for reasons to hope. They are ready to make an act of faith—if they encounter a compelling witness.

This is one reason why Christians surround death and burial with such an abundance of customs, traditions, and rituals. These vary from culture to culture, but they share a profound evangelistic purpose. They draw people out of their ordinary distraction and help them to focus on the meaning of human life—its origin and value and destiny.

The Christian tradition counts "burying the dead" among the classic "corporal works of mercy," and "praying for the dead" among the "spiritual works of mercy." When we do these things, we make ourselves available to grieve with others, to offer a consoling word, and to point a hopeful way to the future. That way is the way of the paschal mystery.

Those who arrived at the tomb on the first Easter morning were instructed first, to see, and then, to give testimony. The angel said to them, "Do not be amazed! You seek Jesus of Nazareth, the crucified. He has been raised; he is not here. Behold the place where they laid him. But go and tell his disciples and Peter" (Mark 16:6-7).

If we are witnesses to Jesus' salvation, we are called to give our testimony as well.

Questions for reflection and discussion

1. Why is it significant that Jesus came to earth at a particular point in history? What books or movies have made the reality of Jesus and his suffering most memorable for you? Why?

2. Why was Jesus crucified at Passover? How does that help you understand the meaning of Jesus' title "Lamb of God," which we pray at every Mass? How does that title deepen your love for Jesus and his sacrifice?

3. How have your experienced the power of the sacraments in your life? How is your faith strengthened? How are you consoled?

4. Why do Catholic funerals express the hope of resurrection? How can funerals be an evangelizing opportunity?

5. When we die with Christ, we die to sin. When we rise with Christ, we rise to new life. How can faith in the power of Christ's death and resurrection help you to fight the battle with sin in your own life? How can you better live in the freedom Christ won for you?

Looking for more?

▶ On the paschal mystery, see the *Catechism of the Catholic Church*, 542, 571, 654, 1067, 1085, 1104, 1171, 1200, 1239, 1344, 1681.

▶ See the *United States Catholic Catechism for Adults*, chapter 8, "The Saving Death and Resurrection of Christ."

▶ Read the accounts of Jesus' passion in the Gospels According to Luke, chapters 22–24, and John, chapters 19–21.

▶ See *The Gift of Blessed John Paul II: A Celebration of His Enduring Legacy*, chapter 23, "A Real Presence: *Ecclesia de Eucharistia* (On the Eucharist in Its Relationship to the Church)."

Chapter 6

Jesus' Ascension and Second Coming

> He ascended into heaven
> and is seated at the right hand of the Father.
> He will come again in glory
> to judge the living and the dead
> and his kingdom will have no end.

What is the revelation?

[Jesus] said to them, "Go into the whole world and proclaim the gospel to every creature. Whoever believes and is baptized will be saved; whoever does not believe will be condemned. These signs will accompany those who believe: in my name they will drive out demons, they will speak new languages. They will pick up serpents [with their hands], and if they drink any deadly thing, it will not harm them. They will lay hands on the sick, and they will recover."

So then the Lord Jesus, after he spoke to them, was taken up into heaven and took his seat at the right hand of God. But they went forth and preached everywhere, while the Lord worked with them and confirmed the word through accompanying signs.

—The Gospel According to Mark 16:15-20

When they had gathered together they asked him, "Lord, are you at this time going to restore the kingdom to Israel?" He answered them, "It is not for you to know the times or seasons that the Father has established by his own authority. But you will receive power when the holy Spirit comes upon you, and you will be my witnesses in Jerusalem, throughout Judea and Samaria, and to the ends of the earth." When he had said this, as they were looking on, he was lifted up, and a cloud took him from their sight. While they were looking intently at the sky as he was going, suddenly two men dressed in white garments stood beside them. They said, "Men of Galilee, why are you standing there looking at the sky? This Jesus who has been taken up from you into heaven will return in the same way as you have seen him going into heaven."

—The Acts of the Apostles 1:6-11

What does it mean?

Jesus' ascension into heaven is one of the most significant moments in his life. For Catholics, Ascension is a great feast day, a solemnity, and a holy day of obligation. We are required to go to Mass so that we can celebrate this mystery. The Church wants to make sure that the whole family is gathered for such a great event.

The Ascension brings to a conclusion the earthly life of Jesus, but it also opens up for us the earthly life of the Church. He ascends in his visible body to make way for his mystical body.

It is important because of what it says to us. We profess that Jesus is the eternal Son of God, the Word become flesh; he is Light from Light, God from God. The Son of God came among us, born of the Virgin Mary. He grew up in a family as one of us; he taught us, he died for us, and he rose from the dead. In his earthly life, Jesus was Emmanuel, "God with us," as present and visible and audible as a next-door neighbor. But now he has completed that chapter. God's presence in Jesus—in his natural human body—has come to an end. So where has that body gone?

In the Ascension we see that Jesus has returned to the Father in glory. In his sacred humanity he has risen in glory to reign in heaven. He has brought the salvation of humanity to a new level, so to speak. He has "divinized" human flesh.

Jesus' real physical human body is now risen and glorified; it is no longer with us. So we look to the empty tomb, and we know the body is risen and gone. We look for no other place where we would find that risen body here on earth because the Ascension tells us that Jesus has returned in glory to his Father.

Yet the New Testament presents this event, not as merely as an ending, but as a beginning. It is the concluding episode in the Gospels of Mark and Luke, but it is the opening story in the Acts of the Apostles, the story of the early Church. As one chapter closes, another opens. Jesus' risen body is with the Father in glory. On earth the body of Christ will be his Church, alive in the Holy Spirit. You and I are members of that body; Christ is our head. The Church, his spiritual body, is where we now find Christ.

Throughout his public life, Jesus knew that his ministry would be completed in this way. On one occasion, he asked his disciples, "What if you were to see the Son of Man ascending to where he was before?" (John 6:62). At his Last Supper, he said plainly, "I am going to the Father and you will no longer see me" (16:10). Even after his resurrection, he told Mary Magdalene not to cling to him, "for I have not yet ascended to the Father" (20:17). Thus, he foretold that his ascension would be the precondition of a lasting communion between himself and his people. In the Church, by means of the sacraments, we cling to him still today.

The New Testament shows Jesus in his ascension as a king at his enthronement and a priest entering the holy place, the sanctuary. To modern minds, this may seem a contradiction in terms, but we must remember that the Old Testament King David and Solomon, the son of David, were both priest-kings. In the Ascension we see Jesus entering into his kingdom as the awaited messiah: both priest and king, the ultimate Son of David.

Our King came not to establish an earthly theocracy extending over a small parcel of ancestral lands inhabited by a few tribes. His mission is far greater than that: "The one who descended is also the one who ascended far above all the heavens, that he might fill all things" (Ephesians 4:10). For that purpose— for the fulfillment of everything—he built his Church and set it on a rock foundation, universal in its reach. He established a kingdom inviolable and incorruptible, over which he will reign forever from heaven.

A Universal Mission

The Church's universal mission is clear from the New Testament accounts of Jesus' ascension. "Go into the whole world and proclaim the gospel to every creature," he tells his disciples in Mark's Gospel (16:15). In the Acts of the Apostles, we find him saying, "You will be my witnesses . . . to the ends of the earth" (1:8). The apostles celebrated this great commission in the most poetic terms: "Undeniably great is the mystery of devotion, / Who was manifested in the flesh, / vindicated in the spirit, / seen by angels, / proclaimed to the Gentiles, / believed in throughout the world, / taken up in glory" (1 Timothy 3:16).

In the Letter to the Hebrews, the emphasis is more on Jesus' priesthood. There we read that Jesus is the greatest priest in all of history. The Temple priests offered the blood of bulls and goats; Jesus, the Son of God, offers his own body and blood, and he offers it on our behalf. "For Christ did not enter into a sanctuary made by hands, . . . but heaven itself, that he might now appear before God on our behalf" (Hebrews 9:24). Thus, we learn that Jesus ascended into heaven for the same reason he died and rose from the dead. He did it all *for our sake*: "He became the source of eternal salvation for all who obey him" (5:9). It is the Ascension that makes his offering possible, and it also makes it perpetual. The Ascension shows him as the priest who entered the holy place and "offered one sacrifice for sins, and took his seat forever at the right hand of God" (10:12). This sacrifice, the offering of his body and blood, is what we share whenever we celebrate the Holy Mass. Jesus is the principal celebrant at every Mass, but he invites our participation.

In the mystery of the Ascension, we celebrate the glorification of Christ, the completion and crowning of his work, but in a certain sense, we also celebrate our own willingness to take up that work. We are to be witnesses to everything Christ revealed—everything he himself had received from the Father! Jesus told his friend Nicodemus: "The one who comes from above is above all. The one who is of the earth is earthly and speaks of earthly things. But the one who comes from heaven [is above all]. He testifies to what he has seen and heard, but no one accepts his testimony" (John 3:31-32).

Jesus came from the Father and revealed to us some things we could never have known. He revealed to us the Father's name. He taught us who God is and who we are in relationship to God. He also taught us that God loves us in a way that we cannot even begin to imagine. To show us how intense that love was, Jesus was prepared to die for us—to hang on a cross, suffer, and die for us.

All of this was part of his revelation. He lived as we do in order to show us how we should live. At the Ascension he tells his apostles that it is now their turn to live the life of Christ in the world. They know that it is an impossible task. But he reassures them with the promise of the Holy Spirit. He will send God's Spirit to live in them and act in them, to give them everything they need. It is the Holy Spirit that makes the Church the living body of Christ.

I love St. Luke's account of what happens next. While the apostles "were looking intently at the sky," he says, "suddenly two men dressed in white garments stood beside them. They said, 'Men of Galilee, why are you standing there looking at the sky? This Jesus who has been taken up from you into heaven will return in the same way as you have seen him going into heaven'" (Acts 1:10-11).

The apostles are standing there, jaws dropping in amazement, and the angels tell them, in so many words: "Don't just stand there—do something! You have your commission. Do what you've been told to do."

Those words are addressed to you and to me. We have inherited the task of those first disciples. Why are we standing idle when we have so much to do? Each one of us can do something positive to manifest the kingdom of Christ—to make it visible and present in the world today. Each one of us can take on some aspect of spreading the kingdom of God, of bearing witness to what Jesus came to reveal. Some can teach. Some can give example. All of us can live the Christian message. Ultimately, the Ascension is directed to you and to me as a challenge.

In Catholic tradition, Jesus' ascension is always connected with his return in glory. He reigns over all things from heaven, and he comes to us bodily in the Mass, but we believe he will return in glory and subject all things to himself. We await this day in joyful hope. For us it cannot be a cause of anxiety. We watch for the day, knowing that even now, he is with us always and will remain so to the end of our earthly days.

How can this truth transform me?

Knowing that Jesus our King is in heaven should free us to live confidently in the world. The Ascension shows us that Christ reigns *even now* over the whole universe. We're not putting our faith in a political leader, who might let us down. Jesus watches over history. He watches over creation. And he watches over my life and yours. He wants the best for each one of us, the way we want the best for our closest family members. If we are firm in faith—if we abandon ourselves to trust in Jesus—we will know his peace even in the midst of difficulties and trials. He will deliver us the peace of heaven. He will give us his strength.

How do I live it?

Some people in the Church are called to spend their earthly days contemplating heaven. God calls them to be hermits or cloistered religious. These are special vocations reserved for a few.

Most of us, however, are commissioned to deliver the good news to the ends of the earth. That is most especially the role of the laity. Jesus sent his disciples to "every creature" (Mark 16:15) and to the "ends of the earth" (Acts 1:8). It is important for us to remember that the earth is round, not flat, and so it has no ends—or rather, it ends at any and every point. The "end of the earth" is the place where you live. It's the place where you work. It's the place where you socialize and spend your leisure time. As an archbishop, I cannot reach those places or the people you meet there. The pope cannot reach those places or people. Nor can your parish priest. God has commissioned *you* to be Christ, to be his body to all the "ends of the earth" in which you find yourself.

Don't just stand there, the angels tell us as we look up at heaven. Jesus has told us to do something. What will you do in response?

Maybe you're already doing something, but you could do more. Maybe you're already doing too much, and you need to focus your efforts to do things better.

Maybe it's time for a reevaluation of how well you and I are responding to our Lord's "great commission." The work we do for Christ is not just another line on our tax returns. It's not just a line on the résumé under "volunteer work." It's our great commission. It's the work of Christ's body on earth today.

How do I share it with others?

Christ wants us to be his body in the world. His body is recognizable in a crowd. He said this at his ascension: "These signs will accompany those who believe: in my name they will drive out demons, they will speak new languages. They will pick up serpents . . . , and if they drink any deadly thing, it will not harm them. They will lay hands on the sick, and they will recover" (Mark 16:17-18).

Exorcists are not the only Christians who drive out demons. You do too—whenever you live prayerfully and act charitably. Your presence is the presence of Jesus Christ. You dispel darkness by your words and deeds. The "serpents" and "scorpions" of the spiritual life flee from your kindness and your attentiveness to others. You help people to heal from the wounds and hurts they've suffered in their souls from their own sins and the sins of others.

Do as Jesus would do. Speak encouraging words. Refrain from gossip. Be patient. Say the hard thing that needs to be said. Lead people back to church. Invite them to the sacraments, especially the Sacrament of Reconciliation.

Questions for reflection and discussion

1. How can you be the presence of Jesus in simple and practical ways in your family? In your parish? In your workplace and neighborhood? How does this make God's kingdom more visible in the world today?

2. Jesus is King of the universe and reigns in heaven, so we can put our trust in him. Why do we often find it so difficult to trust in Jesus completely? What might you do, specifically, to make trusting a little easier?

3. How often do you think about Jesus' Second Coming? Does it cause you anxiety? Or do you wait in joyful hope? Why or why not? How does the Catholic view of the Second Coming differ from how others may view it?

4. What "demons" and darkness around you can you dispel by your words and deeds? When have you seen this happen? Where might you like to see it happen?

5. As the body of Christ in the world today, why is it important to refrain from gossip and to speak encouragingly? Why is it important to speak the truth in love? Why do we often struggle in these areas?

Looking for more?

▶ Read St. Luke's first account of the Ascension in Luke 24:45-53.

▶ Learn about our Lord's Ascension in the *Catechism of the Catholic Church*, 659–672.

▶ See the *United States Catholic Catechism for Adults*, chapter 13, "Our Eternal Destiny."

▶ See *The Gift of Blessed John Paul II: A Celebration of His Enduring Legacy*, chapter 13, "Sowers of the Seed: *Redemptoris Missio* (The Mission of the Redeemer)."

Chapter 7

The Holy Spirit

> *I believe in the Holy Spirit, the Lord,*
>   *the giver of life,*
> *who proceeds from the Father and the Son,*
> *who with the Father and the Son is adored*
>   *and glorified,*
> *who has spoken through the prophets.*

What is the revelation?

But as it is written:

> "What eye has not seen, and ear has not heard,
> and what has not entered the human heart,
> what God has prepared for those who love him,"

this God has revealed to us through the Spirit.

For the Spirit scrutinizes everything, even the depths
of God. Among human beings, who knows what pertains to a person except the spirit of the person that is
within? Similarly, no one knows what pertains to God
except the Spirit of God. We have not received the spirit
of the world but the Spirit that is from God, so that we

may understand the things freely given us by God. And we speak about them not with words taught by human wisdom, but with words taught by the Spirit, describing spiritual realities in spiritual terms.

—St. Paul, First Letter to the Corinthians 2:9-13

What does it mean?

God surpasses human reason. The greatest human mind founders on the Trinity. It's not that God is irrational, but rather that God surpasses our reason; and that, in itself, is a reasonable notion. Any god we could "figure out" would be necessarily less than we are. Such a god would be incapable of creating us and unworthy of our worship.

We can arrive at the existence of God simply by using our reason. Philosophers demonstrate God's existence using "proofs" and "demonstrations," unaided by divine revelation. But we could never know God's *inner life* if it had not been revealed to us. We could never ponder our way to the fact that our one God is a Trinity of divine Persons: Father, Son, and Holy Spirit.

In Christianity's first generation, St. Paul met ardent disciples of Jesus who were somehow still in the dark about the fundamental doctrine of God.

Paul traveled through the interior of the country and came (down) to Ephesus where he found some disciples. He said to them, "Did you receive the holy Spirit when you became believers?" They answered him, "We have never even heard that there is a holy Spirit." (Acts 19:1-2)

There is indeed a Holy Spirit. St. Paul not only taught the doctrine to those believers in Ephesus; he baptized them, and they *received* the Holy Spirit.

We know that there is a Spirit because Jesus has revealed the Spirit to us, just as he has revealed the Father to us. And he has done still more: he has *given* us the Spirit to be our life. That is the reason why God took up our human nature: to share divine life with us. That is the endpoint of our salvation: the sharing of God's Spirit.

In the Creed we profess belief "in the Holy Spirit, the Lord, the giver of life." This is implicit in our action every time we make the Sign of the Cross—every time we sign ourselves "in the name of the Father, and of the Son, and of the Holy Spirit."

Yet many Christians today, like those ancient disciples in Ephesus, lag in their understanding of the third Person of the Blessed Trinity. The Holy Spirit seems, perhaps, to demand more of us because we lack experience of an earthly analogy or reference point. We have, or at least have witnessed, some experience of human fatherhood, so we feel we know something of the Father. The Son became human and lived among us, so we feel we know something of the Son. But what about the Spirit? We are spiritual beings and we have a spiritual life; but we are not inclined, by our fallen nature, to be attentive to it. We must make an effort. We must look more closely at what God has revealed.

Revelation was a gradual process. It came first through mighty acts of divine power. God impressed upon Israel, "I, the LORD, am your God, and there is no other" (Joel 2:27). Thus, it became clear that there is one God. Then God sent his only-begotten Son, his Word, into our world, and Jesus revealed God's fatherhood to us and his own eternal sonship. Finally, as Jesus prepared to return to his Father, he promised to send the Holy Spirit to live with his disciples as Advocate, Consoler, Gift, and Love.

God's gradual revelation was complete when Jesus announced the Father, the Son, and the Holy Spirit. We can find this revelation most clearly and completely in Jesus' so-called farewell discourse in St. John's Gospel, chapters 14, 15, and 16. Jesus is getting his disciples ready for his departure. He has ordained them to be leaders of his Church, and yet they are clearly not ready. That very night they show themselves to be fearful, ambitious, and a bit obtuse.

Yet Jesus gives them the ultimate reassurance. He says this: "I will ask the Father, and he will give you another Advocate to be with you always, the Spirit of truth, which the world cannot accept, because it neither sees nor knows it. But you know it, because it remains with you, and will be in you. . . . The Advocate, the holy Spirit that the Father will send in my name—he will teach you everything and remind you of all that [I] told you" (John 14:16-17, 26). A little later, Jesus adds: "When he comes, the Spirit of truth, he will guide you to all truth. He will not speak on his own, but he will speak what he hears, and will declare to you the things that are coming" (16:13).

In the farewell discourse, it is clear that the Spirit is not a *something*, but a *Someone*, a Person coequal with the Father and the Son, who lives in relationship with the Father and the Son. It is clear, moreover, that this Spirit possesses the fullness of divine wisdom and power—and that the Spirit will hereafter be given to believers. Through this gift, believers will share in God's infinite life, wisdom, power, and love.

The Outpouring of the Holy Spirit

Throughout his ministry, Jesus made clear that the Spirit would be essential to the life of his disciples, as individuals and collectively, as the Church. He said, "No one can enter the kingdom of God without being born of water and Spirit" (John 3:5). Thus, he foretold the gift of the Spirit in the Sacrament of Baptism. He also poured out this gift on his Church as it assembled. After his resurrection he appeared to the apostles, and "he breathed on them and said to them, 'Receive the holy Spirit'" (20:22). We witness the outpouring of the Spirit in a dramatic and visible way, however, in the Acts of the Apostles, in St. Luke's account of the first Christian Pentecost.

> When the time for Pentecost was fulfilled, they were all in one place together. And suddenly there came from the sky a noise like a strong driving wind, and it filled the entire house in which they were. Then there appeared to them tongues as of fire, which parted and came to rest on each one of them. And they were all filled with the holy Spirit and began to speak in different tongues, as the Spirit enabled them to proclaim. (Acts 2:1-4)

Through all the action and drama in the rest of the Book of Acts, the apostles draw their strength from the Spirit. St. Luke shows that the Spirit speaks through the apostles and directs their movements. The Holy Spirit gives them words, courage, zeal, and wisdom for discernment. So pervasive is this divine character in the drama of Acts that the book has sometimes been called "the

Gospel of the Holy Spirit." Acts is the history of the Church. It tells the story of Christianity's first few years, but it also illustrates the principles by which the Church will always live and move forward. The Church lives by the Holy Spirit of God.

Spiritual writers since St. Augustine have spoken of the Holy Spirit as the "soul" of the Church, the Church's life and power. The Church is Christ's new body, but it now lives and moves by the power of the Holy Spirit. The Spirit, who is the eternal principal of unity and life in the Trinity, now gives life and unity to the Church.

The Holy Spirit empowers us—individually and as the Church—to do what needs to be done. The first Christians were a small band with no great resources, and yet they managed to conquer the world for Christ. At the beginning of the Book of Acts, we see them as timid, frightened people, feeling alone and inadequate because Jesus had returned to the Father and left them with an impossible task. Then they receive the Spirit, and soon they are achieving the impossible, incrementally, at God's pace, with God's power.

So it is with the Church today. The Church continues to receive that great Pentecostal outpouring of the Spirit, and the Church continues to bestow the Spirit through the sacraments established by Jesus Christ. As the Spirit was poured out on the apostles, so the Spirit comes to the Church today through the apostles' successors, the bishops, and is shared with the whole body of Christ. The gift of the Spirit comes with baptism; the Sacrament of Confirmation brings about a completion of this initial grace.

It is the Spirit who enables us to share the life of the Trinity even now, in this life, here on earth. We are children of God because we live in communion with God's eternal Son. How is this possible? "God sent the spirit of his Son into our hearts, crying out, 'Abba, Father!'" (Galatians 4:6). "The Spirit itself bears witness with our spirit that we are children of God" (Romans 8:16). The life of a child of God, like the eternal life of the Son of God, is simply life in the Spirit.

Someday the fullness of divine goodness will be manifested, when Christ comes to claim all that is his and to bring it to completion. In the meantime, the Spirit is at work in the Church—and, therefore, at work in each one of us—gradually bringing about God's kingdom in our world.

How can this truth transform me?

The Spirit is always at work in the world and in your life. The Spirit has transformed you and is transforming you. Whether or not we are aware of it, "the Spirit too comes to the aid of our weakness; for we do not know how to pray as we ought, but the Spirit itself intercedes with inexpressible groanings" (Romans 8:26). Every prayer we pray—no matter how inarticulate—we pray in the Spirit, who "intercedes for the holy ones according to God's will" (8:27). The Holy Spirit takes whatever is present but as yet unformed in our desires, makes it complete, and raises it as prayer. When we live in the Spirit, our wants and our needs, our plans and our hopes fall into line with the will of God. Nothing and no one can transform us as thoroughly—and all for the better—as the Holy Spirit.

How do I live it?

We cannot love someone we do not know. We should take steps to grow in our love for the Holy Spirit. As in any relationship, we should seek to know more about the One we love. To that end, we can prayerfully study the relevant passages in the Sacred Scriptures and the *Catechism of the Catholic Church*.

We grow in love when we express our love. We should take advantage of the Church's rich tradition of devotion to the Holy Spirit. Many Catholics say the brief prayer "Come, Holy Spirit" many times during an ordinary day. They offer it as their prayer whenever they need wisdom for decisions or discernment, or when they need courage to do or say something that's challenging or intimidating. Jesus taught us to do this. He said, "Do not worry about how you are to speak or what you are to say. *You will be given at that moment what you are to say.* For it will not be you who speak but *the Spirit of your Father speaking through you*" (Matthew 10:19-20, emphasis added).

The phrase "Come, Holy Spirit" is the shorthand version of a longer responsory prayer. It's good for us to recite that traditional prayer in its entirety every so often.

Come Holy Spirit, fill the hearts of your faithful
    and kindle in them the fire of your love.
V. Send forth your Spirit, and they shall be created.
R. And you shall renew the face of the earth.
Let us pray. O, God, who by the light of the Holy Spirit,
    did instruct the hearts of the faithful, grant that by the

same Holy Spirit we may be truly wise and ever enjoy his consolations. Through Christ Our Lord. Amen.

The Church also teaches us many hymns that we can sing whenever we feel confused or afraid and in need of divine help. I grew up with the hymn "Come, Holy Ghost." Younger generations have been raised with the Spirit-filled songs of the Catholic Charismatic Renewal. There's an old saying, often attributed to St. Augustine: to sing is to pray twice. Once, twice, three times—it is always good for us to sing for the gift of the Holy Spirit.

If we read the Acts of the Apostles, we'll learn to be attentive to the promptings of the Spirit and docile to the direction of the Spirit. We want to be as spiritually responsive as the first Christians were. We want to have the effect and influence they had on their world.

Some Christians find yet another way of devotion in the Acts of the Apostles. They see that through the days that stretched from Jesus' ascension to the coming of the Spirit at Pentecost, the apostles "devoted themselves with one accord to prayer" with the Blessed Virgin Mary (Acts 1:14). Christians today still observe those nine days as a "novena"—a nine-day chain of prayer for the gift of the Holy Spirit. There are many ways to do this. Some prayer books offer formal prayers for this novena. We may also observe it by simply reciting the traditional responsory (on the opposite page) once a day.

In any event, we should celebrate Pentecost as a great and festive day. It is the day the Church dedicates as a solemnity to the Holy Spirit every year.

How do I share it with others?

From the Holy Spirit we receive peace, serenity, and wisdom. These gifts are meant for sharing. If people remark on our ability to keep cool under difficult circumstances, we should let them in on our secret: devotion to the Holy Spirit, life in the Spirit.

We should also be dutiful about praying to the Holy Spirit—quickly, silently, in our hearts—whenever we give witness to our faith, whenever we find ourselves in the midst of an unexpected conversation about the faith. Remember Jesus' promise: the words will be given to us; the Spirit will speak through us.

Questions for reflection and discussion

1. Do you feel that you have a relationship with the Holy Spirit? Do you pray to the Person of the Holy Spirit? Why or why not? At what times might you call on the power of the Spirit to help you?

2. According to St. Paul, how does the Holy Spirit pray and intercede for us (Romans 8:26-27)? Do you sense his presence when you pray?

3. How did the Spirit empower the apostles and the early Church? How can we be as spiritually responsive as the first Christians were?

4. Have you ever felt prompted by the Holy Spirit to say or do something that you might not have thought of on your own?

What happened? What helped you to listen to the Spirit in that situation? What might help you to better listen to the Spirit's promptings in the future?

5. We receive the Spirit in the Sacraments of Baptism and Confirmation, but the graces of these sacraments are still at work in our lives. How might you go about asking God for more of the Spirit?

Looking for more?

▶ To see the Holy Spirit in action, read the entire book of the Acts of the Apostles. Watch for the Spirit's role.

▶ To understand the consequences of life in the Spirit, read chapter 8 of St. Paul's Letter to the Romans.

▶ To learn more about the Person of the Holy Spirit, study the *Catechism of the Catholic Church*, 687–747. To learn more about the Holy Spirit's role in your baptism and confirmation, see 1213, 1215, 1262, 1265–1266, 1285–1321.

▶ See the *United States Catholic Catechism for Adults*, chapter 9, "Receive the Holy Spirit."

▶ See *The Gift of Blessed John Paul II: A Celebration of His Enduring Legacy*, chapter 8, "Lord and Giver of Life: *Dominum et Vivificantem* (The Holy Spirit, Lord and Giver of Life)."

The Church

> I believe in one, holy, catholic and
> apostolic Church.

What is the revelation?

I am writing you about these matters, although I hope
to visit you soon. But if I should be delayed, you should
know how to behave in the household of God, which is
the church of the living God, the pillar and foundation
of truth.

—St. Paul, First Letter to Timothy 3:14-15

What does it mean?

The Catholic faith has been entrusted to the Church. If we
want to call ourselves Catholic, then we have to open our
hearts to God's word and accept what the Lord has said. It is
not enough just to *say*, "I believe in Jesus." We have to *show*
that we believe his words. We have to live by them. And it is
Jesus' words that lead us to believe in a particular Church,
with a recognizable form—a Church that is one, holy, catholic, and apostolic.

Jesus knew that the time would come when he would return to the Father, but he would not leave the Church vulnerable. He would not leave his people as orphans (John 14:18). He established the Church and assumed it would be permanent and identifiable (Matthew 16:18; 18:17). He gave it a certain form. He instituted its leadership and inaugurated its ritual worship (Luke 22:19).

Jesus instituted the Church to carry on his work. He passed on to his apostles the tasks that were his own. He commissioned them to teach in his name, to make disciples, to baptize, to heal, to expel demons, to forgive sins, and to render judgments over the actions of the believers entrusted to their care.

In the Acts of the Apostles, the book that picks up where the Gospels leave off, Jesus promises his apostles, "You will receive power when the holy Spirit comes upon you, and you will be my witnesses . . . to the ends of the earth" (Acts 1:8). In the following chapters, we watch it all fall into place, all under the guidance of the Holy Spirit—and, as Roman Catholics, it looks very familiar to us. The early Church's life is centered on the celebration of the Eucharist: "They devoted themselves to the teaching of the apostles and to the communal life, to the breaking of the bread and to the prayers" (Acts 2:42). The leaders in the Church fall into certain categories. The Scriptures speak of the "bishop" (1 Timothy 3:2), from the Greek *episkopos*, which is also translated as "overseer." There are "presbyters" (James 5:14), from the Greek *prebyteros*, also translated as "priest/ elder." And there are "deacons" (1 Timothy 3:8), from the Greek *diakonos*, also translated as "servants."

Over all these orders of clergy and all the lay members of the Church, the role of Peter continues in the Church in the ministry of his successor, Bishop of Rome, the Holy Father the Pope. Throughout the Book of Acts, we see Peter, the first pope, acting consistently in his role as chief shepherd and universal pastor.

Peter must act as a "Father" because the Church is a family. The New Testament letters of St. Peter and St. Paul repeatedly refer to the Church as a "household" (Ephesians 2:19; 1 Timothy 3:15; 1 Peter 4:17). Its members look to God as Father and see their clergy as representing God's fatherhood in the Church on earth. St. Paul told the Corinthians, "I became your father in Christ Jesus through the gospel" (1 Corinthians 4:15). All earthly fatherhood, including the clergy's, takes its name from God: "For this reason I kneel before the Father," St. Paul wrote to the Ephesians, "from whom every family in heaven and on earth is named" (3:14-15). The word for "family" is *patria*, which means simply "fatherhood," the role that defined the ancient family.

The Church is a family, a household. Its members see one another as brothers and sisters (Colossians 1:2). We share a common birth in baptism. We share a common table in the Eucharist. We hold ourselves to a higher standard of care for one another.

Our family is identifiable—there is a family resemblance. Our Church bears certain "marks"—visible signs of the invisible Spirit. We say in the Creed that the Church is "one, holy, catholic and apostolic." Let's take a closer look at those terms.

The Church Is One

The Church is one because it is Christ's body, and a living body must be unified. If it is divided, it dies. Christ stood in the midst of his apostles and disciples as one integral person: God, but man as well. So it is in his Church. There is one Church, and it is heavenly and earthly. We do not separate Christ and his saints in glory from believers who are still struggling here on earth. The Church is one as his body is one. If there are fractures in that body—if there are divisions among people who claim Christ as Lord, if there are divisions about the way people understand the revelation and the Creed—it is not by Jesus' will. Today within the Church, the ecumenical movement works to unify all Christian believers who are divided one from another, to restore what Christ intended for his Church from the beginning.

The Church Is Holy

Why do we say the Church is holy when we know better? You and I look at ourselves and at one another, and we know that we fail. Even the greatest saints in history made frequent use of the Sacrament of Confession. There is an undeniable measure of sin in the world and even in the lives of very good Christians. So why do we dare to say the Church is "holy"? We can say it because the Church is the enduring presence of God, of the Holy Spirit, of Jesus Christ. In the Church God is with us, always, until the end of time (Matthew 28:20), and so the Church in its fullness is holy. It is holy with the holiness of the Holy Spirit, who sanctifies us even though individual members may not live up to that gift. "Christ loved the church and handed himself over for her to *sanctify* her,"—that is, make her holy (Ephesians 5:25-26, emphasis added). He made the Church "a holy nation" (1 Peter 2:9). Its members on earth, though sinners, are called to be "holy ones," or saints (Colossians 1:2).

The Church Is Catholic

The Church was born of the Spirit on the first Christian Pentecost, and from that first moment, it was multicultural and inclusive—that is, it was *catholic*, a word that comes from the Greek, *katholikos*, which means "universal." From the day the Church was born on that first Pentecost, we see a congregation made up of many ethnicities: "Parthians, Medes, and Elamites, inhabitants of Mesopotamia, Judea and Cappadocia, Pontus and Asia, Phrygia and Pamphylia, Egypt and the districts of Libya near Cyrene, as well as travelers from Rome, both Jews and converts to Judaism, Cretans and Arabs" (Acts 2:9-11). That is a snapshot of the world's first universally welcoming family. Jesus excluded no one based on race, nationality, gender, class, or other worldly status. His Church is meant to embrace everyone. Ours is not a national church. The Catholic Church does not pledge allegiance to any one flag. Christ looks at us all in the same way. We are all sinners in need of redemption, and that is what entitles us to membership in the Church and a relationship with Jesus Christ. In our desire to be saved, to be forgiven, to be redeemed, we come to Christ in his Church, and all are welcome.

The Church Is Apostolic

The Catholic Church is apostolic because it has a continuous relationship—a continuous and verifiable continuity—with the apostles who were the first witnesses to Jesus Christ. Jesus never wrote a book; he summoned *apostles*—particular men who would bring the gospel to the ends of the earth, until the end of the age. Moreover, he promised to be with them. Needless to say, those apostles have since gone on to their heavenly reward. But their work was taken up by successors. We see this already in the New Testament, as the apostles replaced members who had died (Acts 1:15-26) and named new leaders for mission churches (1 Timothy 3:1-7). The process has continued through the millennia. We have never broken the chain of succession. Today, as in the first century, the bishops are the visible manifestation of this apostolic element in the Church. The task of the bishop is to teach, to lead, and to sanctify—to carry on the work of Christ as head of his Church in the midst of a world that seeks the presence of God. The bishops' job is to speak for the Church, to be a personal and visible point of reference, and to verify and authenticate that the message we proclaim today is the very same message the apostles received from Jesus.

One, holy, catholic, and apostolic: the Church possesses these qualities because of its communion with Jesus Christ. They are graces, gifts of divine life. Yet each of these signs also has a human dimension with human imperfections. In fact, the effectiveness of the signs is sometimes compromised by the scandals that arise from the sinfulness of the members of the Church, both clergy and laity. So throughout history, the marks of the Church have a paradoxical aspect. The Church is one, and yet we find divisions. The Church is holy, and yet its members are sinful. We attest to the universality of the Church, and yet we see instances of exclusion and prejudice.

The Church, the body of Christ, is composed of flesh and Spirit. The Church is made up of you and me, members who are frail, fragile, failing—but, at the same time, possessed of a divine gift. We hold God's grace, the Holy Spirit, sacramental power, yet we hold it all in earthen vessels. This paradox will be with us until the end. We know that we are not yet living the fullness of the life of Jesus Christ. Yet we know too that he urgently wants us to share that life.

Jesus made extravagant promises to the Church. It would be inviolable, built on a rock foundation; it would be invested with power; it would be his presence. He is still fulfilling those promises today, every day, in the Church, in your diocese, in your parish, and in your home.

So then you are no longer strangers and sojourners, but you are fellow citizens with the holy ones and members of the household of God, built upon the foundation of the apostles and prophets, with Christ Jesus himself as the capstone. Through him the whole structure is held together and grows into a temple sacred in the Lord; in him you also are being built together into a dwelling place of God in the Spirit. (Ephesians 2:19-22)

How can this truth transform me?

Make yourself at home. When individual Catholics travel or move to a new city, they know where they will worship. They are not consumers in a religious marketplace. God did not come to earth to establish a shopping mall. Catholics are children of God and members of God's household. We go to the Catholic Church.

Thus, we are free from the anxieties of inventing the Christian faith. It has already been done, once for all, by Jesus, and he entrusted the faith, with all its dogmas and mysteries, to the apostles and their successors. They have protected it, preserved it, and passed it on—in spite of persecution and the enmity of the world, the flesh, and the devil. The gates of the netherworld have not prevailed, and they will not. The Church has never altered or abandoned the doctrine of Jesus Christ.

So we don't have to bear the burden of figuring out from scratch what the Church has known since the very beginning. Is God a Trinity? Is the Eucharist really Jesus? How many orders of clergy are there? How shall we be saved? Should babies be baptized? What does baptism do? Outside the Catholic Church, different people offer competing and mutually contradictory answers to these questions.

Catholics know that they can find Christ in his Church and that the Church will give them Christ's definitive answers. Catholics can look to Christ in his body and say, like St. Peter, "Master, to whom shall we go? You have the words of eternal life" (John 6:68).

This is security. Catholics don't go "church shopping." We know that we're in a family, and family members have faults, but our security is at home. Our inheritance is in the family. Our lot is with our people. We believe *in* the one, holy, catholic, and apostolic Church.

How do I live it?

We need to treasure unity and work for it. A true Catholic has no "denominational spirit" or "party identity." Our Church is not one among many, but rather the one that includes the many. We should strive to be unifiers, who bring the straying and wavering back to the joy and confidence that come with the practice of our faith.

We acknowledge differences in order to overcome them. We make distinctions so that we can unite people unnecessarily opposed. In order to be peacemakers and unifiers, we must have a strong and deep knowledge of Catholic doctrine. We cannot share what we do not first possess. Unless we feed ourselves, we will not have the strength to feed others. We need to make time for study and be disciplined about it. The best ecumenism is carried forward by those who know and love the tradition that has been entrusted to them.

Within the Church we need to live as a family. When we talk about our pastor or about fellow parishioners, we should not speak as if we're complaining about our car or our outdated household appliances. These people are family to us. They are father, mother, brother, and sister to us (Matthew 12:49-50). They are the body of Christ to us. Sometimes, as Blessed Mother Teresa of Kolkata used to say, they are "Christ in distressing disguise." They should call forth our kindness.

The ancient Roman world converted because individual pagans looked at Christians and said, "See how they love one another." Our love within the Church is our strongest witness.

This doesn't mean that we have to don our rose-colored glasses when we go to a parish council meeting. It doesn't mean that we can never raise an objection to the pastor. It does, however, mean that we are obliged to speak the truth in love. If someone in the Church is doing something wrong, embarrassing, or harmful, we need to speak up so that we can help avoid potential scandal. Jesus gives good guidelines for doing this:

> "If your brother sins [against you], go and tell him his fault between you and him alone. If he listens to you, you have won over your brother. If he does not listen, take one or two others along with you, so that 'every fact may be established on the testimony of two or three witnesses.' If he refuses to listen to them, tell the church. If he refuses to listen even to the church, then treat him as you would a Gentile or a tax collector. Amen, I say to you, whatever you bind on earth shall be bound in heaven, and whatever you loose on earth shall be loosed in heaven. Again, [amen,] I say to you, if two of you agree on earth about anything for which they are to pray, it shall be granted to them by my heavenly Father. For where two or three are gathered together in my name, there am I in the midst of them." (Matthew 18:15-20)

Our tradition refers to this kindly interaction as "fraternal correction," the kind of help that one brother or sister gives to another. It is familial and helpful, whereas gossip and grumbling are divisive and corrosive. Correction unites Christians; gossip only divides.

The apostles gave us good models for living this way. St. Paul found himself in the unenviable position of having to correct St. Peter (Galatians 2:11-14). He did so without rancor, and St. Peter responded without defensiveness. This, too, is a model for us. When people correct us, we should receive their words with gratitude and serenity.

How do I share it with others?

Invite your friends to worship. Non-Catholics sometimes have mistaken ideas about the Church, and they imagine Catholic worship to be very different from what it really is. Take them along with you on a Sunday or even on a weekday. Make sure to prepare them first; non-Catholics cannot, for example, receive Holy Communion, and there is a helpful explanation of that restriction included in most missals. But they will still find much that will impress them or make them think.

Some non-Catholics believe that our Church neglects the Sacred Scriptures. When they go to Mass, however, they learn that there is more Scripture in Catholic worship than in the Sunday gatherings of most other Christians.

Some people watch the news or read the papers and believe that the Catholic Church is full of bitter people divided against one another and angry at the hierarchy. When they go to Mass, however, they encounter a community. It may not be perfect, but it's clearly functional. And it is more truly inclusive and diverse than any other voluntary community on earth. One novelist,

James Joyce, described the Church accurately as "here comes everybody."

The Mass speaks for itself and speaks for Christ. So does our community. As a Catholic who is faithful to the tradition of the apostles, so do you.

So share the moment that is most important in your life. Share your worship. Let your friends see you pray. Give them an opportunity to join you in prayer, as they feel comfortable doing so.

Questions for reflection and discussion

1. Sometimes we hear people say, "I am spiritual but not religious." Usually they mean that while they believe in God, they don't participate in the life of a church. Is it possible to call yourself a Catholic and not participate in the life of a parish community?

2. What do you find most attractive about the Church? What do you find most meaningful about the Catholic life we share? What are some common misconceptions you encounter?

3. Were you ever tempted to leave the Church? If so, what made you stay? Have you ever asked a convert what led them to find their home in the Church?

4. Why is it so important to think of the Church as a family? How does this make you think and feel about your fellow parishioners?

5. Is there someone in your life whom you can invite to join you at Mass or for a special liturgy at your parish? Have you ever shared with a colleague at work or a friend something from a good homily you heard or something that your parish was doing that you thought was important or made you proud? What was the person's reaction? Has it become easier to talk about your faith and life at the parish with others?

Looking for more?

▶ The *Catechism of the Catholic Church*, in 748–975, offers a thorough teaching on the Church.

▶ See the *United States Catholic Catechism for Adults*, chapter 10, "The Church: Reflecting the Light of Christ"; and chapter 11, "The Four Marks of the Church."

▶ Read about the Church in the Scriptures: Acts 9:31-43; Acts 14:20-28; Acts 16:4-5; 1 Corinthians 4:12-17.

▶ See *The Gift of Blessed John Paul II: A Celebration of His Enduring Legacy*, chapter 2, "Handing on the Faith: *Catechesi Tradendae* (On Catechesis in Our Time)"; chapter 19, "A Priceless Gift: *Vita Consecrata* (The Consecrated Life)"; and chapter 24, "Good Shepherds: *Pastores Gregis* (The Bishop, Servant of the Gospel of Jesus Christ for the Hope of the World)."

Chapter 9

One Baptism, One Body in Christ

> *I confess one Baptism for*
> *the forgiveness of sins.*

What is the revelation?

I . . . urge you to live in a manner worthy of the call you have received, with all humility and gentleness, with patience, bearing with one another through love, striving to preserve the unity of the spirit through the bond of peace: one body and one Spirit; . . . one Lord, one faith, one baptism; one God and Father of all, who is over all and through all and in all.

But grace was given to each of us according to the measure of Christ's gift.

—St. Paul, Letter to the Ephesians 4:1-7

As a body is one though it has many parts, and all the parts of the body, though many, are one body, so also Christ. For in one Spirit we were all baptized into one body, whether Jews or Greeks, slaves or free persons, and we were all given to drink of one Spirit.

Now the body is not a single part, but many. If . . . an ear should say, "Because I am not an eye I do not belong to the body," it does not for this reason belong any less to the body. If the whole body were an eye, where would the hearing be? If the whole body were hearing, where would the sense of smell be? But as it is, God placed the parts, each one of them, in the body as he intended. If they were all one part, where would the body be? But as it is, there are many parts, yet one body. The eye cannot say to the hand, "I do not need you," nor again the head to the feet, "I do not need you." Indeed, the parts of the body that seem to be weaker are all the more necessary, and those parts of the body that we consider less honorable we surround with greater honor, and our less presentable parts are treated with greater propriety, whereas our more presentable parts do not need this. But God has so constructed the body as to give greater honor to a part that is without it, so that there may be no division in the body, but that the parts may have the same concern for one another. If [one] part suffers, all the parts suffer with it; if one part is honored, all the parts share its joy.

Now you are Christ's body, and individually parts of it. Some people God has designated in the church to be, first, apostles; second, prophets; third, teachers; then, mighty deeds; then, gifts of healing, assistance, administration, and varieties of tongues. Are all apostles? Are all prophets? Are all teachers? Do all work mighty deeds? Do all have gifts of healing? Do all speak in tongues? Do all interpret? Strive eagerly for the greatest spiritual gifts.

—St. Paul, First Letter to the Corinthians 12:12-31

What does it mean?

In baptism we receive the gift of the Holy Spirit, and we are united so closely to Christ that we are identified with him. We are one with him, and his life is our life. This is the ancient faith of the Church. Listen to the words St. Augustine preached more than a millennium and a half ago: "Let us rejoice then and give thanks that we have become not only Christians, but Christ himself. Do you understand and grasp, brethren, God's grace toward us? Ponder and rejoice: we have become Christ."[13]

Through baptism we have come to share in Jesus' life and death. We were "buried with him," said St. Paul (Romans 6:4), and in Christ we arise to a new life. It is a divine life, because we are partakers of his "divine nature" (2 Peter 1:4), as he has partaken of our human nature. We arise from the baptismal waters fit for heaven.

Thus, in the Creed, we profess belief in a baptism "for the forgiveness of sins." We read in the Book of Revelation (21:27) that "nothing unclean will enter" heaven. Sin is incompatible with God's life. Baptism washes away all our sins and so becomes the precondition for our new life. Forgiveness is a great gift, and it is a prerogative of God alone (Mark 2:7), but God wants to give us still more than that. The Father wants us to live as his children—to live in Christ, with the very life of the Son of God.

St. Augustine marveled that the Father and the Son have shared with us their own bond of love. The very bond that unites the Trinity unites us with the Trinity—and unites us together with one another. We are one in the Spirit. With the gift of the Holy Spirit, first at Pentecost but ever after in baptism, the Church is enlivened, and it is one. "Through that which is common to the Father and the Son . . . we have communion with one another and with Them. . . . By that gift we are reconciled to the Divine and made to delight therein."[14]

From the moment of our baptism, the Spirit of God's Son cries out in our own souls: *Abba! Father! Daddy!* (Romans 8:15 and Galatians 4:6). Every prayer that arises in us comes from this impulse of the Spirit.

The Person who unifies the Trinity unifies us with one another in love in the Church. Look again at the reading at the beginning of this chapter from St. Paul to the Ephesians. We have one body and one baptism, one Spirit, one Lord, one faith, and one Father. He could not be more emphatic about the gift of unity and about its importance.

The Radical Equality of One Baptism

St. Paul's favorite image of this unity is the human body, which is also Christ's body. Paul returns to it again and again in several of his letters. Just as the parts of our body are interdependent, God willed for us in the Church to depend upon one another. We need one another. So there are no class divisions in the Church. There is neither Jew nor Greek, slave nor free, male nor female. Though we each receive a different role, we all enjoy radical equality in the one baptism.

Baptism is a new birth because we receive new life and we pass from the old order—the old creation bound up in sin, ignorance, and separation from God—into a whole new creation in which we are now alive in the Spirit with a new life and freed from sin. God's Spirit gives us a new, truly spiritual life.

To undergo baptism, then, is not just the matter of a moment. It involves a personal commitment to live a certain kind of life, a divine life amid ordinary human circumstances. For those who are baptized as infants, the parents and sponsors (godparents) make that commitment and pledge to raise the child accordingly. For those who receive baptism in adulthood, there is a longer process by which the Church confirms the commitment of the new believer, who makes several public declarations of the intention to live the Christian life.

Baptism may be received only once in a lifetime. The essential Rite of Baptism is simple: the priest or deacon pours water over the new Christian, water that has been blessed for the sacrament. As he does so, he says, "I baptize you in the name of the Father, and of the Son, and of the Holy Spirit." There are other elements to the ritual—anointings and prayers, the lighting of a candle, clothing with a new garment—but the water and the Trinitarian formula are what we call the "matter and form" of the sacrament. The water and the words are the two outward signs of what is transpiring as the new creation unfolds. In almost all cases, baptism is administered by a member of the clergy. However, in a case of dire emergency, such as the danger of imminent death, anyone may baptize. Even a non-Christian may perform a valid baptism, as long as they intend to do what the Church does.

All of this symbolism accomplishes the very thing that it sets out to show us. Sacramental signs, such as the pouring of water and the saying of the words, do not just articulate what we would like to happen; they make it happen. By God's power and grace, they bring about the very transformation they proclaim. Jesus willed this when he commanded his disciples to go out to all the world and baptize.

In the water of baptism, sin—personal and original—is washed away so that we can truly say that we have died with Christ and were buried with him. At the same time, the water signifies an outpouring of the Holy Spirit, God's life-giving spirit, that brings us to a new and elevated level of life, where we can say we have also risen with Christ. The new life implanted in our hearts through the outpouring of the Holy Spirit in baptism is the life of God—a divine seed planted within us that needs to be nurtured, nourished, and cultivated so that it can grow and flower into life everlasting.

It is the matter of a moment, and yet the moment endures for a lifetime and then for an everlasting afterlife. Baptized into Christ, we must live *now* in grace, and our lives should be a reflection of that grace, a Christian witness to what has happened. We have become children of God.

Jesus did not need to be baptized "for the forgiveness of sins." He was sinless. But he underwent baptism nonetheless, and he did so for many reasons. The early Fathers of the Church said that he descended into the waters in order to sanctify them—to sanctify all the waters of the world—to be fit for all of us to be baptized.

In his baptism, Jesus also modeled for us the entryway to divine life. Baptism is an image of new birth—an emergence from waters. The Gospel accounts of Jesus' baptism make clear that the event at the Jordan River manifested Jesus' origin with the Father. As we say in the Creed, he is "born of the Father before all ages." At the Jordan, the signs of his Trinitarian life are the voice of the Father declaring Jesus to be his "beloved Son" (Mark 1:11) and the descent of the Holy Spirit (in the form of a dove, John 1:32). Jesus' baptism in the Jordan is the image on earth of a heavenly communion: the eternal life of the Blessed Trinity.

The *Catechism of the Catholic Church* speaks about our own baptism as a "plunge" into the water, symbolizing "the catechumen's burial into Christ's death, from which he rises up by resurrection with him, as 'a new creature'" (1214). These words pick up a theme in the New Testament—found, among other places, in the Second Letter of Paul to the Corinthians, where we are told that "whoever is in Christ is a new creation" (5:17).

Just as in the beginning, when God created everything and sent his Spirit to form out of nothing everything that was to be, so in his new creation God sends forth the Spirit to bring forth a whole new level of life in each believer—the life of God's own Spirit. There is a real parallel between the first creation and this new and marvelous creation of the Spirit. Baptism, then, is not just a personal initiation into the Church, but rather a continuation of the new creation coming to be all around us and in us through the power of the Holy Spirit.

The new creation is quite unlike the old, which has been hobbled and frustrated by the effects of sin. God's new creation proceeds in a peaceful, fruitful way. It is alive and coherent, and its movements are providentially coordinated. It is like a healthy body—Christ's body.

As members of the Church, we are beset by human imperfections, but whatever our shortcomings, the very soul of the Church is the Holy Spirit. Each follower of Christ, every believer, is anointed in the Spirit through the Sacrament of Baptism. Everything the Church is and has to offer begins with the Sacrament of faith—Baptism.

The Work of the Laity

By far, most of the members of the Church are the laity. They are laywomen and laymen baptized into Christ and confirmed in the gifts of the Spirit. The Second Vatican Council defined the work of the laity as taking up "the renewal of the temporal order as their own specific obligation."[15] The temporal order is our world, our culture, our neighborhoods, our workplaces, our families, our friends.

The fact that we are baptized should make a difference, not only in our personal lives, but in our world. When something happens in the community or when laws are enacted challenging some of our most cherished convictions, bishops and priests will often hear the question, "Why doesn't the Church do something about this?" While it is true that the clergy are called to proclaim the gospel, it is equally true that laywomen and laymen are challenged to apply the gospel to the circumstances of our time. The immense task of addressing the serious social and moral problems of our society cannot be left to the Church's hierarchy. Everyone has to be involved and take an active role. We sometimes hear politicians say that while they may hear from bishops and priests on specific issues, they do not hear much from the Catholic laity.

The principle of lay involvement holds for other areas as well. The voice of Catholic physicians needs to be heard in the area of medicine. Catholic lawyers need to speak out on the ethics involved in the law. Catholic parents need to be involved in education issues. The list goes on. This is what the Second Vatican Council meant when it said that laypeople are responsible for "the renewal of the temporal order."

Laypeople have responsibility for the temporal order because it requires all the knowledge, skills, talents, and insights that they acquire and exercise in their varied secular areas of work. The temporal order must be renewed with reverence by those who respect its own "stability, truth, goodness, proper laws and order," as the Second Vatican Council said,[16] while bringing it into conformity with the higher principles of Christian life.

Laywomen and laymen clearly are essential to the transmission of the gospel. All the faithful are called to participate in the evangelization and sanctification of the temporal order. The voice and the engagement of the laity will ultimately determine the direction of our society. Bishops have the responsibility to teach, but the laity must apply that teaching, and they must also witness to its validity by their actions and conversations with others.

The final words of the Mass, "Go in peace," are not just a dismissal but a commissioning—a renewal of Christ's great commission. They are a sending forth of those in attendance to bring our Lord to a world that needs him desperately. Through our baptism we have come to possess the life of the Lord. We cannot live that life unless we live it as Jesus did in his flesh. We cannot keep his life unless we give it to others, unless we share it.

Hear again the words of the great commission: "*You* will receive power when the holy Spirit comes upon *you*, and *you* will be my witnesses," Jesus said, "to the ends of the earth" (Acts 1:8, emphasis added).

How can this truth transform me?

How do you view your spiritual life, and how does it relate to what you do all day, every day of the week? Our religion is not something relegated to Sunday worship. It is pervasive, and we need to cultivate a continual awareness of God's presence and action in us and through us. Some people feel dissatisfied or frustrated because their workdays seem drab compared to their times of prayer. A deeper understanding of our baptism, however, can transform our workdays themselves into acts of prayer.

A traditional Catholic way of doing this is by reciting a prayer, or "Morning Offering," when we wake up. There are many different forms for such prayer. This version was popular when I was a child, and has remained so:

O my God, I offer you all of my prayers, works, joys and sufferings of this day, for your greater honor and glory, in reparation for my sins, in thanksgiving for all you have given me, for the intentions of my family and friends, and in particular for the intentions of our Holy Father. Amen.

Through the grace of our baptism, we are transforming the world around us. However, we tend to forget this fact as we go about our everyday business and ordinary life. Yet we are the ones who offer the world to God. We do it in Christ because we have been baptized into his life. It is good for us to bring this amazing truth to mind at the beginning of each day, even if we are still groggy with sleep, and then renew our offering through the day, whenever we think of it or whenever we need a reminder or need a boost.

How do I live it?

In baptism we have been given *all things* in Christ (Romans 8:32). We are to judge *all things* with Christ (1 Corinthians 2:15). God's "plan for the fullness of times" is "to sum up *all things* in Christ" (Ephesians 1:10, emphasis added), until *all things* are "subjected" to him (1 Corinthians 15:28) and reconciled to him (Colossians 1:20) in "the times of universal restoration" (Acts 3:21).

Those times are now, and God accomplishes the great restoration and reconciliation through your life and mine. When you go to work, people depend upon you—co-workers, customers, clients, patients, and students. If you work at home caring for a loved one who is ill or disabled or for your children, then they are depending on you. When you do your work well for the sake of others and for God, you are living as Christ in the world. You are living the life you have received in baptism.

In baptism we have come to share in Christ's offices of priest, prophet, and king. I have been ordained to the fullness of Holy Orders, and so I serve in a priestly role at the Church's altars. But all laypeople serve in a priestly role *out in the world*. They offer the goods of the world and the work of the world as a sacrifice to the Father. As a bishop, I fulfill a prophetic role as I preach from the pulpit. But all the laity are prophets when they speak the truth in the midst of hostility, when they console the grieving with words of everlasting life, when they speak with love in response to hatred.

Baptized into Christ, we have all entered into his kingship. With Christ we are "heir of all things" (Hebrews 1:2). With our daily work, no matter what we do, we are restoring it to its place in God's plan. We are claiming the world as Jesus' inheritance.

Jesus worked at ordinary jobs in his society. He was a craftsman who worked with his hands. He became a teacher, a rabbi. He even helped his friends in their fishing business. When people saw him work, they said, "He has done all things well" (Mark 7:37). As we live out our days conscientiously and faithfully, people should say the same about all those of us who are baptized into Christ.

How do I share it with others?

Perhaps you know people who say they respect Jesus as a great moral teacher but don't see the need to accept his claim to be God and to belong to his Church. You can help them to realize that Jesus taught morality as a consequence of divine life—a life that he shares with us in baptism. Through the actions of baptized believers, the kingdom of Christ breaks into the world and changes it for the better.

Maybe you also know Christians who feel dissatisfied with their work. Perhaps they consider themselves to be underemployed or unappreciated, or perhaps they are feeling frustrated with a lack of opportunity. You can help them to accept God's will and to seize the opportunity of living as Christ in the present moment. You can help them to see their work in a different light, a divine light—the light of the baptismal candle.

God calls some people to be active in their parish's program for the Rite of Christian Initiation of Adults (RCIA). They serve as teachers, companions, and sponsors. They answer a lot of questions. It is a rewarding task, preparing people for the fullness of Christ's life in the sacraments. If you believe this is God's call for you, make some time to talk to your pastor.

Questions for reflection and discussion

1. Unity is very important in our relationship with Christ and in our life in the Church. What does unity mean in a spiritual way? What does it mean in a practical way? What is one thing you could do to promote unity in the Church?

2. What was the most memorable baptism you ever attended, and why? How did it increase your appreciation of the sacrament?

3. How is your life different because of your baptism? How do you continue to nurture and cultivate the seed of faith that was placed in you at baptism?

4. How does a deeper understanding of our baptism transform our work in the world? Why is your work and what you do each day important to God and to his kingdom?

5. How is morality a consequence of the divine life within us, the life that Christ shares with us in baptism? Do you approach moral issues differently when you see them in such a light?

Looking for more?

▶ The *Catechism of the Catholic Church* gives a stunning exposition of the meaning and practice of baptism in 1213–1284.

▶ See the *United States Catholic Catechism for Adults*, chapter 15, "Baptism: Becoming a Christian."

▶ Read about the Church as Jesus' body in Acts 9:4-5; Romans 12:5; 1 Corinthians 12:12-27; Ephesians 3:6; 4:12; 5:23; and Colossians 1:18, 24; and also in the *Catechism of the Catholic Church*, 787–796 and 805–808.

▶ See *The Gift of Blessed John Paul II: A Celebration of His Enduring Legacy*, chapter 10, "Building a Better World: *Sollicitudo Rei Socialis* (On Social Concern)"; and chapter 11, "Speak and Live the Faith: *Christifideles Laici* (The Vocation and the Mission of the Lay Faithful in the Church and in the World)."

Eternal Life

*I look forward to the resurrection of the dead
and the life of the world to come. Amen.*

What is the revelation?

When Jesus arrived, he found that Lazarus had already been in the tomb for four days. Now Bethany was near Jerusalem, only about two miles away. And many of the Jews had come to Martha and Mary to comfort them about their brother. When Martha heard that Jesus was coming, she went to meet him; but Mary sat at home. Martha said to Jesus, "Lord, if you had been here, my brother would not have died. [But] even now I know that whatever you ask of God, God will give you." Jesus said to her, "Your brother will rise." Martha said to him, "I know he will rise, in the resurrection on the last day." Jesus told her, "I am the resurrection and the life; whoever believes in me, even if he dies, will live, and everyone who lives and believes in me will never die. Do you believe this?" She said to him, "Yes, Lord. I have come to believe that you are the Messiah, the Son of God, the one who is coming into the world." . . .

So Jesus, perturbed again, came to the tomb. It was a cave, and a stone lay across it. Jesus said, "Take away the stone." Martha, the dead man's sister, said to him, "Lord, by now there will be a stench; he has been dead for four days." Jesus said to her, "Did I not tell you that if you believe you will see the glory of God?" So they took away the stone. And Jesus raised his eyes and said, "Father, I thank you for hearing me. I know that you always hear me; but because of the crowd here I have said this, that they may believe that you sent me." And when he had said this, he cried out in a loud voice, "Lazarus, come out!" The dead man came out, tied hand and foot with burial bands, and his face was wrapped in a cloth. So Jesus said to them, "Untie him and let him go."

—The Gospel According to St. John 11:17-27, 38-44

There was a rich man who dressed in purple garments and fine linen and dined sumptuously each day. And lying at his door was a poor man named Lazarus, covered with sores, who would gladly have eaten his fill of the scraps that fell from the rich man's table. Dogs even used to come and lick his sores. When the poor man died, he was carried away by angels to the bosom of Abraham. The rich man also died and was buried, and from the netherworld, where he was in torment, he raised his eyes and saw Abraham far off and Lazarus at his side. And he cried out, "Father Abraham, have pity on me. Send Lazarus to dip the tip of his finger in water and cool my tongue, for I am suffering torment in these flames." Abraham replied, "My child, remember that you received what was good during your lifetime while Lazarus likewise received what was bad; but now he is comforted here, whereas you are tormented. Moreover, between us and you a great chasm is established to prevent anyone from crossing who might wish to go from our side to yours or from your side to ours." He said, "Then I beg you, father, send him to my father's house, for I have five brothers, so that he may warn them, lest they too come to this place of torment." But Abraham replied, "They have Moses and the prophets. Let them listen to them." He said, "Oh no, father Abraham, but if someone from the dead goes to them, they will repent." Then Abraham said, "If they will not listen to Moses and the prophets, neither will they be persuaded if someone should rise from the dead."

—The Gospel According to St. Luke 16:19-31

What does it mean?

The Church traditionally speaks of four "last things": death, judgment, heaven, and hell. In the Creed we allude to our earthly life's ending, but we speak of it as a beginning, as something we "look forward to." This seems a strange thing for us to say. As human beings, we have a natural instinct to preserve our lives, and so we have a natural dread of death. As Christians too, we love our earthly life because it is a great gift from God.

Yet we were made for something greater. We were made to live an eternal life in heaven, where "there shall be no more death or mourning, wailing or pain" (Revelation 21:4). Heaven is the new life implanted in our hearts through the outpouring of the

Holy Spirit in baptism. Heaven is the fullness of the life of God. At baptism we receive that divine nature as a seed planted within us. It needs to be nurtured, nourished, and cultivated so that it can grow and flower into life everlasting. God gives us the grace to achieve that growth, from moment to moment over the course of a lifetime; but every one of us is free to accept this gift, neglect it, or even reject it and end that life in Christ altogether.

It is Jesus who marks out his own. In the Sacrament of Baptism, the minister—bishop, priest, or deacon—claims the one to be baptized for Christ. He marks the baptized with a seal that indicates our permanent vocation, the call by Jesus Christ—a call to life everlasting.

The Scriptures state clearly that God wants our destiny to be with him: a communion of Father and child that is so great that it is beyond our imagining. To St. Paul, heaven is "what eye has not seen, and ear has not heard, / and what has not entered the human heart, / what God has prepared for those who love him" (1 Corinthians 2:9). St. John speaks of it in similar terms: "Beloved, we are God's children now; what we shall be has not yet been revealed. We do know that when it is revealed we shall be like him, for we shall see him as he is" (1 John 3:2).

The path to such glory begins with our baptism, but it continues through our earthly lives by our growth in virtue and our sacramental life.

Under Judgment

Our earthly life ends in death, and death is the occasion of judgment. But in reality, we are always under judgment. To live in God's presence is to live under judgment. We know that our Father in heaven holds us to the highest standards, and he gives us the grace to meet those standards. When we are aware of God's presence, we know that we are not God, and we are aware of the aspects of our lives that do not line up with his holy will. During our earthly life, we may live in denial of this fact. We can distract ourselves and put off the changes we really need to make. We can defer repentance indefinitely. In death, however, we are freed from such illusions and distractions, "for we shall see him as he is," and then we shall see ourselves in divine light (1 John 3:2). To stand in judgment is to see ourselves as we truly are and to know whether or not we have lived up to God's grace—to know whether we have fashioned a life fit for heaven.

For someone who has rejected or neglected God's grace, even a moment in the divine presence would be unbearable. Such souls, during their earthly lives, have distanced themselves so far from God that separation has become habitual and preferable. Such permanent separation from God is the very definition of hell. This is what the *Catechism* tells us:

> We cannot be united with God unless we freely choose to love him. . . . To die in mortal sin without repenting and accepting God's merciful love means remaining separated from him forever by our own free choice. This state of definitive self-exclusion from communion with God and the blessed is called "hell." (1033)

As much as we might prefer to deny it, hell is a reality. Scripture speaks of this everlasting punishment and warns us against the deliberate malice that destroys a person from within and leads to eternal death. Christ spoke often of hell. He described it as "the unquenchable fire" (Mark 9:43; cf. Matthew 25:41; Luke 16:24). He spoke with compassion, to warn us away from the ultimate tragedy (cf. Mark 9:43-50), of the "second death" (Revelation 21:8), with its permanent separation from the everlasting life in God, for which we were made (Matthew 25:31-34). Jesus spoke forcefully in the images used in that time of "Gehenna, where 'their worm does not die, and the fire is not quenched'" (Mark 9:47-48). In doing so, our Lord called us to conversion. He warns that those who deliberately persist in malice face a horrible end.

Still, we know that God is merciful. "All wrongdoing is sin," but not all sin is mortal (1 John 5:17). Not all sin brings about a complete separation from God. Some people die in grace and in the friendship of God, but burdened with lesser sins, *venial sins,* and imperfections that mar their spiritual life. The Church teaches that their souls are cleansed in a purgation that prepares them to enter into the presence of God. The *Catechism of the Catholic Church* tells us that "the Church gives the name *Purgatory* to this final purification of the elect, which is entirely different from the punishment of the damned" (1031). This teaching finds a solid foundation in Scripture, which speaks of the practice of praying for the dead. In the Second Book of Maccabees, we encounter the tradition of offering prayers for those who have died so that they might be cleansed of their sins: "Thus he [Judas Maccabeus] made atonement for the dead that they might be absolved from their sin" (12:46).

The precise form of this purgation has never been defined by the Church. Certainly, a part of the pain is the temporary separation from God, yet it is a suffering that can be borne knowing that ultimately it will end. St. Augustine asked God to purify him in this life so that it would not be necessary for him to undergo purification after death, in purgatory, which he described as cleansing fire.

Those who come to eternal life will enjoy every manner of blessing, but at the core of their joy will be the possession of God himself. No longer shall we see God merely by faith, but we shall see him "face to face" (1 Corinthians 13:12). This blessed union with God brings us perfect peace and is far more than simply seeing or knowing God. In God's gracious gift of life everlasting, we will rejoice in God's infinite goodness. It is in that expectation that we pray that we will hear these words of our Lord at our own judgment: "Come, share your master's joy" (Matthew 25:21).

We know that death is not simply an ending but also a beginning. The Letter to the Hebrews describes Jesus as our leader and exemplar. He suffered, he died, and he rose again. We, too, shall rise again in our bodies. Scripture makes this abundantly clear. St. Paul says, "We do not want you to be unaware, brothers, about those who have fallen asleep, so that you may not grieve like the rest, who have no hope. For if we believe that Jesus died and rose, so too will God, through Jesus, bring with him those who have fallen asleep. . . . Therefore, console one another with these words" (1 Thessalonians 4:13-14, 18).

Such words are indeed a consolation. The resurrection of Christ is a pledge that we, too, will rise one day. All of Christianity turns on this truth, this promise. "If there is no resurrection of the dead, then neither has Christ been raised. And if Christ has not been raised, then empty [too] is our preaching; empty, too, your faith" (1 Corinthians 15:13-14).

Death, judgment, and purification are hard things to contemplate. But the resurrection and heaven make such contemplation worthwhile and salutary. To know the options God has placed before us is to live with true freedom. God gives us the liberty to accept his love or reject it, for true love depends on such freedom, "the glorious freedom of the children of God" (Romans 8:21).

How can this truth transform me?

Clarity about the "last things" is very helpful in ordinary life, even for people who are very young. If we have a healthy awareness of our common destiny, we can order everything in life toward that end. We can order our loves and we can order our fears.

Some people pursue earthly goals based on their desire for bodily comfort and pleasure. They say they love life, but they really love pleasant sensations. They know that death and suffering are inevitable, and so they avoid those things at any cost—even at the cost of committing sins. It is better, they believe, to seek immediate gratification than to bet on distant heaven.

Christians, however, seek transformation. They know the demands of bodily desires, but they seek to subject them to grace, spiritual discipline, and divine law. They pursue bodily health because they know that the human body is a gift from God. But their wish for health is subordinate to their faith in heaven. Their love for comfort is subordinate to their love for God. Their fear of illness is subordinate to their fear of displeasing God. Their fear of death is subordinate to their fear of the "second death," which is hell. Fear is not the best motivation for doing the right thing, but it's not a bad one either, and we do need all the help we can get.

An awareness of the last things helps us to choose wisely and confidently as we make our way through life. We know that we are always in God's presence, and so always under judgment. Such constant awareness about ultimate things gives us a rare clarity as we face immediate and urgent decisions.

Faith is a wake-up call. "Therefore, stay awake, for you know neither the day nor the hour" (Matthew 25:13). God calls us to live life abundantly, whether we are young or old. Christ wants us to enjoy a love that lasts forever, and he wants us to begin our heaven now, even in our earthly life, by staying close to him.

How do I live it?

Catholic tradition teaches us many ways we can anticipate God's judgment and prepare for it. We can spend a few minutes examining our conscience before going to bed. As we see the moments when we should have done better, we can tell God we are sorry by making an Act of Contrition:

O my God, I am heartily sorry for having offended you, and I detest all my sins, because I dread the loss of heaven and the pains of hell, but most of all because they offend you, my God, who are all good and deserving of all my love. I firmly resolve, with the help of your grace, to confess my sins, to do penance, and to amend my life.

This prayer is good because it is forward-looking. It says that, as long as we have life, we will strive to improve; we will try to love more.

We should also make regular use of the Sacrament of Reconciliation. We should confess our sins to a priest. The Church asks us to go to Confession at least once a year, but we should really go more often than that. Confession gives us a chance to make an honest accounting of our lives and receive God's forgiveness, and it also gives us the grace to overcome the sins that trouble us.

All of these practices make for a better life—better for us and better for those who have to live and work with us. A good life is the best preparation for death and judgment.

We prepare for death by all our prayers because, in reality, prayer is the life of heaven. Every time we pray the Hail Mary, we ask the Blessed Mother to "pray for us sinners, now and at the hour of our death." Another time-honored Catholic custom is to ask St. Joseph to intercede that we may have a death like his own—in the presence of Jesus and Mary:

O blessed Joseph, who gave up your last breath in the arms of Jesus and Mary, obtain for me this grace: that I may breathe forth my soul in praise, saying in spirit, if I am unable to do so in words: "Jesus, Mary, and Joseph, I give you my heart and my soul." Amen.

There are many traditional prayers for this purpose. We may also use our own words to ask for the same grace.

How do I share it with others?

In everyday life, we can help people become aware that there are long-term consequences to their actions. Pleasure is not the same thing as happiness. True happiness is blessedness. True happiness is love that endures forever. Immoral pleasure is fleeting, and when it passes, it leaves a sinner more miserable than ever.

We can be a great help to friends and family members who are dying. Rather than distracting them from their condition, or just denying it outright and avoiding what is undeniably a difficult topic of conversation, we should try to be available and open so that they are able to speak frankly about it with us. We should try to help them prepare in a realistic and hopeful way. We should make opportunities for them to talk to a priest, to make their confession, and to receive Communion and sacramental Anointing of the Sick.

Questions for reflection and discussion

1. Catholics differ from one another in their thoughts about a "happy death." Some say they hope to go quickly, to minimize temptations to despair. Others say they hope for a longer time to prepare for judgment. How can you be best prepared for any eventuality?

2. How can we order our lives so that our priorities line up with God's and so that we are seeking him, the source of all joy,

rather than transitory pleasures? Are there any changes you need to make so that your life is better ordered toward God?

3. How does regularly examining our consciences and going to Confession help us live a better life, one without regrets when we are dying? How does it increase our awareness of the four "last things": death, judgment, heaven, and hell?

4. Do you "look forward" to having a resurrected body? What do you think it will be like?

5. Have you ever spent time with someone who was dying? Was that person open to hearing about God? How were you able to help him or her? What did you learn?

Looking for more?

▶ For Catholic doctrine on the "last things," see the *Catechism of the Catholic Church*, 988–1060.

▶ See the *United States Catholic Catechism for Adults*, chapter 13, "Our Eternal Destiny"; and chapter 18, "Sacrament of Penance and Reconciliation: God Is Rich in Mercy."

▶ For the Scriptures on the resurrection and the life to come, see Acts 17:32; 1 Corinthians 15:12-26; 1 Thessalonians 4:13-18; Revelation 20:11 to 22:17.

▶ See *The Gift of Blessed John Paul II: A Celebration of His Enduring Legacy*, chapter 6, "Sin and Forgiveness: *Reconciliatio et Paenitentia* (Reconciliation and Penance)."

Chapter 11

The Beginning

When I was very young, every Mass ended with the "last Gospel." The priest proclaimed the same reading every single day, and it was St. John's beautiful prologue: "In the beginning was the Word, / and the Word was with God, / and the Word was God" (1:1).

Every Mass ended with a new beginning.

I think this book, too, should end with a beginning—because the Church these days is insistently telling us that the Holy Spirit wants to start something new. God wants to work a new wonder in you and me. The popes for many years have been calling this movement of the Spirit the "New Evangelization."

Pope John Paul II first used the term as he called for a renewal of the first evangelization of the Americas, a task that began in 1492. Pope Benedict XVI has echoed the summons and often compared it to the first evangelization of Europe, which began two thousand years ago.

We are tasked with a New Evangelization, but clearly the popes are not thinking of it as a short-term project. It must become the work of your lifetime and mine. It must then be taken up by the people whom you and I will evangelize. After that, it must become the mission of the people *they* will have evangelized.

This is not merely the work of the clergy. It is the work of the whole Church. The Church, the body of Christ, exists in order to evangelize. Now that you and I are baptized into the body of Christ, *you and I exist in order to evangelize.* It gives meaning to our lives. We cannot be fulfilled apart from fidelity to this call.

Our gifts are many, but they are diverse. You and I will go about our evangelizing in different ways. Each way is integral to God's great plan for history. We cannot tell whose role, if any, will be more important. Only God knows that. We judge by earthly standards. We tend to be impressed by statistics, by "results," and by media notices. But those don't necessarily reflect what God sees. When we all arrive at our judgment, I think we'll be surprised to learn of the contributions that were most important.

I have been a priest for almost a half century and a bishop for about half that time. You could say that I have spent my life preparing this book, through my preaching and teaching. I am bringing it together, however, at a significant moment in history. As I write these words, the Holy Father has declared a Year of Faith and summoned the world's bishops to Rome for a synod on the New Evangelization. It was my privilege to serve as relator general for the synod.

The synod was all about the transforming power of the Catholic faith. The faith once delivered to the apostles still has the power to transform the world, one life at a time—my life and yours, our neighbors' lives, our family members' lives.

We all want to be transformed. We want to change for the better. We want to make commitments and resolutions and keep to them. We want to be the sort of people we admire. Yet we find that change is hard.

We all want our world to be transformed. Any thoughtful person, but especially a Christian, should be moved to prayer when the news is on the television (or the computer screen) or in the morning paper on the table.

It is our task to cooperate with God's grace and bring an abundance of good news, an abundance of the gospel, to a world collapsing in its own misery. We need not resign ourselves to what we have inherited or what we have suffered at the hands of others. God wants to transform you and me by means of the faith. Then he wants us to live that faith and share it with others. That is how he transforms the world.

That's the stuff of the New Evangelization.

• • • • • • •

It all begins with God speaking. "In times past, God spoke in partial and various ways to our ancestors through the prophets; in these last days, he spoke to us through a son, whom he made heir of all things and through whom he created the universe" (Hebrews 1:1-2).

At the heart of the human encounter with the divine is God's communication of his Word. "In the beginning was the Word, / and the Word was with God, / and the Word was God /. . . . And the Word became flesh and made his dwelling among us / and we saw his glory, / the glory as of the Father's only Son, / full of grace and truth" (John 1:1, 14).

Jesus of Nazareth is the Eternal Word who has taken on our human nature so that God might speak to us, and we might hear

God's Word in the words, gestures, and signs that we are capable of hearing, feeling, grasping, and understanding.

On our own we cannot even begin to understand. But it is Christ who comes among us to reveal who God is— our Father!— and, therefore, who we are—his children!

The night before he died, Jesus told his apostles that he would ask the Father and that the Father would give them another Advocate who would abide with them forever. "I will not leave you orphans; I will come to you. . . . The Advocate, the holy Spirit that the Father will send in my name—he will teach you everything and remind you of all that I told you" (John 14:18, 26).

In living continuity since those days, the Church has passed on the words—the words we otherwise would not have—that introduce us to Jesus, to the Jesus of Nazareth who is Mary's Son and God's Son, to Jesus who is the Word come among us to speak to us of the inner life of the Father.

Salvation and grace come to us through Jesus, and now they continue to reach us through his Church. That is why Christ founded his Church. We do not relate to God solely as individuals, but also as members of his family united with Christ. It is through Christ, present and manifest in the Church, that we come to God. Jesus continues to mediate to us in the visible communion that we identify as the one, holy, catholic, and apostolic Church.

To be a Catholic is to recognize the role of the Church, not as incidental or secondary to salvation, but as the very means created and given to us by Jesus so that his work, accomplished in his death and resurrection, might be re-presented in our day and applied to us.

Jesus did not hesitate to identify himself with his Church. To the disciples, as he sent them to preach in his name, he said, "Whoever listens to you listens to me. Whoever rejects you rejects me" (Luke 10:16). To those who did deeds of charity for his little ones, he proclaimed, "Whatever you did for one of these least brothers of mine, you did for me" (Matthew 25:40). Of St. Paul, who had been vigorously persecuting the Church before his own conversion, Christ asked, "Why are you persecuting me? . . . I am Jesus, whom you are persecuting" (Acts 9:4, 5). At the Last Supper, he spoke of the intense unity that makes him one with those who are united by faith and love to him: "I am the vine, you are the branches" (John 15:5). The vine and branches are one living reality. So it is also with Christ and his Church. So it must also be with Christ and you.

• • • • • • •

The popes have spoken of the New Evangelization as a universal call. It is for everyone. In this, they draw from the message of the Second Vatican Council, which spoke of a universal call to the apostolate—and a universal call to holiness.

We cannot be Christians if we do not share our faith. St. Paul said, "Woe to me if I do not preach it!" (1 Corinthians 9:16). We cannot hold on to our faith if we are not looking to spread it. If we think of it as something merely private and personal, we have missed the point. Unless we share what we have been given, we have failed to love, failed in charity, because our world needs our witness—mine and yours.

Our witness must be an overflow of our lives. The saints are evangelizers who bring the Word of God into the world through the witness of their deeds as well as their words. We may not be counted among the canonized saints just yet. But we must strive to be.

"Go, therefore, and make disciples of all nations, . . . teaching them to observe all that I have commanded you" (Matthew 28:19, 20). Jesus has freed us from the power of sin and saved us from death. The Church receives from her Lord not only the tremendous grace he has won for her but also the commission to share and make known his victory. We are summoned to transmit faithfully the gospel of Jesus Christ to the world. The Church's primary mission is evangelization.

So there it is: We must come to know the revelation. We must come to know what it means. We must live it and share it, ask questions, and probe more deeply.

The Blessed Virgin Mary, as Mother of the Church, is Mother of the New Evangelization. She is a model and patron for our efforts. It was because of her faith that the Word of God entered into our world. In imitation of Mary, we can bring about—through our faith and witness to the life of the Spirit—a change in ourselves and a change in the world in which we live.

May Mary, Star of the New Evangelization and example for every disciple, every missionary, and every evangelizer, intercede for us, so that our work may result in abundant fruit for the glory of God and the salvation of all men and women.

We begin, in a small way, with the faithful profession of the Creed. It is only the beginning.

Completed in Rome on October 22, 2012, the Memorial of Pope Blessed John Paul II, Father of the New Evangelization.

Endnotes

1. Pope Benedict XVI, General Audience, May 23, 2012, accessed at http://www.vatican.va /holy_father/benedict_xvi/audiences/2012/documents /hf_ben-xvi_aud_20120523_en.html.
2. Pope Benedict XVI, *Jesus of Nazareth: From the Baptism in the Jordan to the Transfiguration* (New York: Doubleday, 2007), 132.
3. *Ibid.*
4. Pope Benedict XVI, Address to Newly Appointed Bishops, September 15, 2011, accessed at http://www.zenit.org/article -33449?l=english.
5. Pope Benedict XVI, General Audience, May 23, 2012, accessed at http://www.vatican.va/holy_father /benedict_xvi/audiences/2012/documents /hf_ben-xvi_aud_20120523_en.html.
6. *United States Catholic Catechism for Adults* (Washington, DC: United States Conference of Catholic Bishops, 2006).
7. Pope Benedict XVI, *Jesus of Nazareth: From the Baptism in the Jordan to the Transfiguration* (New York: Doubleday, 2007).
8. This audience can be accessed online; see above URL address.
9. Pope Benedict XVI, Angelus Address, August 12, 2012, accessed at http://www.vatican.va/holy_father/benedict_xvi /angelus/2012/documents/hf_ben-xvi_ang_20120812_en.html.

10. *The Gift of Blessed John Paul II: A Celebration of His Enduring Legacy*, Cardinal Donald Wuerl (Frederick, MD: The Word Among Us Press, 2011).
11. St. Augustine, Letter 187.6.20.
12. This audience can be accessed online at http://www.vatican.va/holy_father/benedict_xvi/audiences/2011/documents/hf_ben-xvi_aud_20111221_en.html.
13. St. Augustine, *Tractates on the Gospel of John* 21.8.
14. St. Augustine, *On the Trinity* 15.29.
15. Second Vatican Council, *Apostolicam Actuositatem* 7.
16. Second Vatican Council, *Gaudium et Spes* 36; see also *Apostolicam Actuositatem* 7

 His Eminence Cardinal Donald Wuerl is the Archbishop of Washington and was elevated to the College of Cardinals in 2010 by Pope Benedict XVI. Known for his efforts on behalf of Catholic education, he is a chairman of the United States Conference of Catholic Bishops' Committee on Doctrine and a member of the USCCB Committee on Evangelization. He served as the relator general for the Vatican Synod of Bishops on the New Evangelization for the Transmission of the Christian Faith. He is the author of numerous articles and books, including *The Gift of Blessed John Paul II* and *Seek First the Kingdom*.

The Cardinal was born in Pittsburgh, Pennsylvania, and received graduate degrees from the Catholic University of America, the Gregorian University while attending the North American College, and a doctorate in theology from the University of Saint Thomas in Rome. He was ordained to the priesthood on December 17, 1966, and ordained a bishop by Pope John Paul II on January 6, 1986, in St. Peter's Basilica, Rome. He served as auxiliary bishop in Seattle until 1987 and then as bishop of Pittsburgh for eighteen years until his appointment to Washington. His titular (cardinalatial) church in Rome is Saint Peter in Chains.

the**WORD**
among us®

The *Spirit* of Catholic Living

This book was published by The Word Among Us. For more than thirty years, The Word Among Us has been answering the call of the Second Vatican Council to help Catholic laypeople encounter Christ in the Scriptures—a call reiterated recently by Pope Benedict XVI and a Synod of Bishops.

The name of our company comes from the prologue to the Gospel of John and reflects the vision and purpose of all of our publications: to be an instrument of the Spirit, whose desire is to manifest Jesus' presence in and to the children of God. In this way, we hope to contribute to the Church's ongoing mission of proclaiming the gospel to the world and growing ever more deeply in our love for the Lord.

Our monthly devotional magazine, *The Word Among Us*, features meditations on the daily and Sunday Mass readings, and currently reaches more than one million Catholics in North America each year and another 500,000 Catholics in 100 countries. Our press division has published nearly 200 books and Bible studies over the past 12 years.

To learn more about who we are and what we publish, log on to our Web site at **www.wau.org**. There you will find a variety of Catholic resources that will help you grow in your faith.

Embrace His Word, Listen to God . . .

www.wau.org